Voyage of a Lifetime

By

Paul England

First Edition Voyage of a Lifetime published by L&R HartleyPublishers Murwillumbah NSW 2008

Second Edition Published by Paul England,

Printed by FC Productions, Sydney 2013

ISBN: 978-1-925023-91-6

Contents

Illustrations

Don Caisley

Don and his Volvo Truck

As Don read the morning newspaper, an article about fishermen blocking the channel ports of France caught his eye. Not that striking French fishermen had much relevance here in Australia but that article stirred memories of an old North Sea trawler that had blocked the port of Le Havre for a full day.

The trawler, under the command of a Swede, Lars Eric Ellinson had been hauling a load of gun metal scrap slung under the hull. Lars had salvaged the metal from deep water, but being on his own - his partner had left him after a difference of opinion, had been unable to haul it aboard.

The scrap was secured under the hull with ropes and as each succeeding tide went out, Lars shortened the securing ropes, until he had the scrap close enough to the bottom of the hull to be able to enter harbour where a crane could lift it to the dockside. Unfortunately, he misjudged his load and as he entered Le Havre, grounded Beth across the main entrance to the harbour

The port authorities impounded the trawler after clearing the harbour for shipping and that was where Don came in. He purchased that old trawler – more commonly known as an MFV, or motor Fishing Vessel, for the amount still owing on it by Lars and his partner. Beth was to become his home for more than two years, and take him and his family through more adventures and excitement during that period than most people would expect in a lifetime.

He lavished love and hate on that old MFV in equal amounts. You could almost call it a marriage, and like most marriages, the feelings, whether love or hate, grew day by day. But she never let him down. There were times when she needed coaxing, sometimes she would do exactly the opposite of what was expected of her, like the time in Panama when she rammed the freighter, but when the going was really rough, she could be relied on. He was born June 12th 1929 and christened Donald Bransby Caisley. The MFV was built in Gravarne, Sweden in 1931 and named 'Nordhaven', later changed to 'Beth'.

Don was a man with an ordinary background, childhood, teenager and then a period in the British army after conscription, then back out into civilian life again, marriage and children. What was not ordinary were the facets of his character - ambition, determination and pride. Beth had ordinary beginnings, like Don. She was built of oak, in Sweden, one of many hundreds and indistinguishable from the rest of her sisters. But, unlike her sisters, who remained working in and around the North Sea, Beth was to sail the oceans of the world.

*****

The Idea Is Born

Driving along the A32 through Hampshire, Don felt at ease in his big Volvo truck, blissfully unaware that his life would change forever within the next few days. He was his own boss, owned his own truck and trailer and business was good. He was especially happy on this particular morning. The trip was his third to Europe in one month and that meant a good month for the Caisley family. The trucking business is very competitive, and for Don, one trip to Italy just about covered the bills and two trips meant a little profit. Three trips in the same month was unusual but totally acceptable, as it meant a boost to the family bank balance.

Transcontinental Transport was one of the first companies to make regular runs between England and Southern Italy and it was Don's determination that ensured the success of the company. The cargo he carried varied from mundane foodstuffs - spaghetti and vegetables, to more valuable and exciting items such as coins from the British Government mint to mercury. The value of the cargo was such that on occasions he had received a police escort to Southampton. Don was hauling a mixed cargo on this trip and was bound for the Southern Italian city of Naples. The weather was good and he had no worries as he thought of the journey ahead. Out of Alton and into the Hampshire countryside the big rig rolled on, its diesel engine running smoothly. Don had a good ear for engines and could detect problems just by listening. Like a musician, he could pick a dud note. He knew exactly how the Volvo should sound at various speeds and loads. The truck was his second home, complete with sleeping accommodation.

He tuned the radio, trying to find a local station for a bit of light music and commentary to keep him company. A pop group came on, raucous and unmelodious so he searched the dial for something a bit more civilized. He found a news programme and settled back to driving.

The newsreader droned on with the day's events - nothing very startling, and then he read an item about Britain's proposal to join the Common Market. 'Oh no, not again' thought Don, 'won't they ever come to their senses'. He knew, more than most people in England that the living standard of the average European – having spent so much time in Europe with his trucking business, was well below that of a comparable Englishman. 'Damn Common Market, why can't Britain do something on her own for a change?' It was a pet hate of Don's, and one subject generally guaranteed to make him angry. He listened to the rest of the news and then switched to another station. The truck, all 32 tons of it rolled on towards Southampton. Don knew the road well, having made the same journey many times before. At every landmark, he mentally checked off the remaining time before his arrival at Southampton.

At the docks, he went routinely through all the formalities of customs, weighbridge and the dozen or so other jobs he had to do before he left England with his loaded truck. Once aboard the ferry he relaxed. Soon the ship was underway and Don made his way to the bridge to talk to the captain, as he had done on several previous trips.

It was 1972 and Britain's proposal to join the Common Market was gathering momentum. Such a major event was, naturally, the main topic of conversation among Englishmen - after the weather, so it was inevitable that the two men would eventually discuss the subject. For and against, there were many points of view, but Don would not be persuaded from his anti EC stand. After about fifteen minutes or so the subject turned to other matters and he was happy to be able to forget the Common Market for a while. He always enjoyed the ferry voyage, it gave him a chance to unwind and just meet and talk to people. During the time he had been making the trips he had got to know quite a few of the regular passengers and crew.

The voyage passed swiftly and soon he was driving off the ship and going through the French customs at Le Havre. Standing in line and waiting while a French Customs official fussed over his papers did not please him. He was impatient and wanted to get back on the road, but the formalities were part of the job and he accepted them with resignation.

Eventually all the forms and papers were signed and stamped and he was cleared to go. He collected his passport and the other papers, put them in his briefcase and headed back in his truck. Wasting no time he was soon leaving the port and on the road to Rouen. From Rouen to Paris, then on the auto route to Macon - where he planned to spend the night in his truck. The following morning at first light, he was back on the road to Bourg-en-Bresse, Nantua and Saint Julien-en-Genevois, then to Mont Blanc and the Italian customs.

Italian customs are much like customs anywhere else in the world, except they take a lot longer to fuss over formalities. Don liked to reach them in plenty of time - he planned to make Rome before nightfall and still had over 750 kilometers to go after the border. He counted himself very fortunate when he got back into the Volvo after only two and a half hours. The remainder of the journey took Don through Aosta, Milan, Rome and then Naples.

It was the end of the outward journey but there was no time to relax. The truck had to be unloaded, then after a short rest it was reloaded for the return journey, and then back the way he had come with a load of spaghetti, mostly for his home town of Bedford, which had a large Italian community.

The return journey passed without event and he rolled into the port of Le Havre after making good time. He had a few hours to kill after clearing customs and so he made his way to a bar where he knew he would find a friendly face. He wasn't a habitual drinker but he did enjoy the company. He ordered a beer and took it over to a table where three other drivers were sitting. Don knew only one of them, but that didn't matter, truck drivers are a fraternity, a sort of exclusive club, and whatever the nationality, could always find common ground for conversation. After the usual banter about trucks, women and hitchhikers the conversation turned to the subject that was most topical - the Common Market.

"It should make it a lot easier for us" said one driver. "Customs clearance and all this waiting around couldn't get any worse, and surely the idea is to be able to move goods freely between member countries."

"Perhaps they will make us all drive on the wrong side of the road" said another.

"That and a lot worse", said Don. His views on Britain's entry into the EEC were well known to all the drivers he came into contact with along the route. He was affectionately known as 'Mr. De Gaulle', because his colleagues said that of all his French friends, General De Gaulle was his favorite because he had kept Britain out of the EEC for so long. "Why the hell should we join? What benefit will England get from the EEC? If life and conditions are so much better in Europe than in England,

Just cleared by Italian Customs and ready to continue his journey to Naples

why do you think the ferries and aircraft are always full, taking French and Germans across the channel to do their shopping? They don't flood over there because they like the trip or the weather!" Once Don got on to the subject of Britain's entry to the EEC he was almost unstoppable. "They shop in Marks and Spencers and all the other big stores and buy up by the ton. It's cheaper for them than buying in their own countries. After they have paid the fare, they're still in pocket, and generally the products they buy are of better quality. You ask most French people what they think about the Common Market, and, unless they are farmers, they're not very enthusiastic. First thing you know our living standards will be brought down to the level of the French and Italians." Don waited for a comment from a driver he knew was pro EEC, but there was none. "We got rid of the feudal system way back in the nineteenth century and raised the level of the working class above peasants. There are still people living like peasants in France and Italy, and if that's what we are heading for, you can keep your Common Market."

"Look Don" said the third driver, "there's nothing you or I or anybody like us can do about it. If the Government decides to join, then we join it, like it or not."

"That's maybe your idea," said Don, "but it certainly isn't mine. You can knuckle down and do what the French Government tell you, but I guarantee if England joins, then I'm off to Australia!"

"Come off it Don, you'll still be running spaghetti back for the Italians in Bedford in five years from now. How old are you now, forty odd? You're too old to pull up stumps and move half way across the world."

Don was annoyed. He didn't want to continue the conversation. He had had the same discussion many times before and knew exactly how it would progress. He viewed the average Englishman's opinion of entry to the EEC as apathetic.

"Look lads, I'm going for a bit of fresh air down by the harbour. I'll see you on the ferry". He finished his drink and left the bar.

As he walked alone thoughts of the conversation he had just left filled his mind. *'I've done it again, said I'll go to Australia if England joins the Common Market,'* he thought. He knew – as most people did, that England's membership was almost a foregone conclusion, and his livelihood was threatened. He had said he would go and he meant it. His pride would not let him retract. Some years earlier, when he had been conscripted into the army, a similar thing had happened, and Don had volunteered for the Parachute Regiment rather than retract a statement. That is the sort of man he is!

Don had relations in Australia and was soon thinking positively about the move. The more he thought about it, the more he was sure he would do it. By that time he had reached the harbour wall and was looking over the fishing trawlers and other craft in the harbour. The seagulls were screeching and wheeling overhead and the air was full of the usual fishing port noises. Boats were moving in and out of the harbour and there was a smell of salt and seaweed in the air, but above the ambient noise of the harbour there was an air of tranquility that is peculiar to any fishing port. Don had never had anything to do with the sea – apart from the ferry trips, but like most people, he enjoyed a holiday by the seaside. He recalled some of the earlier seaside holidays with his family. They seemed such a long time ago.His business had kept him very busy over the past few years and had not left much time for vacations. For himself, it didn't matter, but in building the business up, an extra load had been placed on his wife, Lena. Apart from the truck and trailer he owned, Don had also leased another trailer, and while he was hauling one, Lena was arranging the loading of the other. She also looked after the administration side of the business. Don used to arrive home after a trip, grab a handful of money and other necessities and hit the road again. He realised that his single minded attitude to business was not conducive to a good family life, and although Lena and his two boys seldom complained, he had promised that one day he would make it up to them. Maybe going to Australia and starting a new life would be the way to do it.

Don was enjoying the spring sunshine and his soliloquy when a ship's siren jolted him back to reality. He hurried back to the ferry - there were still one or two things he had to do before he could board for the return trip to Southampton and home.

*****

Lena, I've Bought A Boat

Beth, as she was purchased, before the year long refit by Don

The notion of going to Australia had been with Don a long time, as a collection of ideas or dreams, coming and going as he drove across Europe. The subject had been discussed with the family on several occasions, without any decision one way or the other.

The Caisleys lived in the small village of Cranfield, just north of Bedford – the county town of Bedfordshire in England, and like most villages, it was very parochial. Most of the villagers had been born, raised and schooled there, as had their parents and grandparents before them. Everybody knew everybody else and even to contemplate moving to another town would have set tongues wagging a few years previously. Now the whole pattern of village life was changing. New housing estates were springing up, and with them an influx of 'foreigners' – to the villagers anybody who didn't originate from within a ten mile radius of Cranfield was a foreigner.

When Don's sister had emigrated to Australia some years earlier, the local sages had discussed it over their mild and bitters in 'The Swan' - the local watering hole. 'She'll be back, you mark my words'. But of course, she did not come back, and as far as Don could judge from her letters, she and her husband were enjoying their new life in Perth.

Now, with a commitment made, the notion had blossomed into a firm goal. There were a number of ways he could take himself and his family to Australia. He could emigrate with assistance from the Australian Government. This was the most popular way and there was virtually no cost involved. The Government required only £10 per head for the fare, either by sea or air. To Don this was too easy, if there was no effort required then it probably wasn't worth doing, and anyway everybody went that way. It was not original. He thought about driving overland – a few people had done it, but he was not enthused by that idea. From his experience with the truck he knew it was possible to have everything impounded due to a minor infringement in some countries. He couldn't risk that, and besides, the idea of driving was not original either, as far as he was concerned, most of his working life had been spent on the road, behind the wheel of a truck. That left sailing his own boat, and the more he thought about that, the more he warmed to the idea.

Don had never done any sailing before, nor did he have any experience of boats, but as he had often said to his two sons, 'you can do anything if you put your mind to it'. It was his philosophy through life, and part of his character. Sailing his own boat was no longer an option, his mind was made up. The next step was to find a suitable boat and plan the voyage.

To that end, all Don's spare time was spent looking for a craft that would be adequate for the purpose - on the continent in Europe and in England. The boat had to be large enough to accommodate the Caisley family; Don, his wife Lena and their two sons, Peter aged 17 and Jonathan aged nine. It had to be big enough to hold sufficient supplies to sustain the family during the voyage. It had to be an ocean going vessel capable of sailing in the roughest of water. Cost would also be a major factor as the Caisley funds were not unlimited.

The problem was to find a boat that fitted all the requirements. Don looked over boats every time he was near the sea. He scanned advertisements, talked to seafaring people and finally decided on a fishing trawler: Generally known as MFVs, there were many motor fishing vessels for sale. Mostly, they were 40 to 50 years old and redundant because of the decline in the fishing industry, due to the extension of territorial waters.

MFVs are not the sleekest of craft. Constructed of oak and pitch pine they have a rather cumbersome appearance, but they are solid, dependable and among the most seaworthy boats ever built. Designed for trawling in the North Sea, which is notorious for its unpredictable and generally inclement weather, they were able to withstand the heaviest of seas.

There were several MFVs that Don looked at, with prices ranging up to £5000, and with no knowledge of boats he found it difficult to choose from the selection available. Then he remembered seeing an old MFV for sale in Le Havre - not in good condition aesthetically, but basically sound. On closer inspection he noted that the condition was not greatly different from boats of three times the price.

With the help of some of his French friends, Don contacted the owner, a Lars Eric Ellinson, and discussed the boat with him. It turned out that the MFV, Beth - as she was called, had been impounded by the LeHavre harbour authorities for blocking the harbour. Ellinson had been using Beth for salvage work and while towing eight tons of gunmetal slung under the hull, had run aground across the harbour entrance. The boat was jointly owned - the other owner being somewhere in England, and because of a disagreement with his partner, Ellinson had been operating the boat by himself. When Don first saw the old MFV, Ellinson was in trouble with the authorities and Beth had to be sold. The price was £700, providing the joint owner could be located and agreed to the sale.

Beth was built in 1931 at Gravarne in Sweden, and had originally been named 'Nordhaven'. She was 58 feet from stem to stern and 19 feet across the beam. The displacement was 58 tons and she drew 10 to 11 feet of water. During the Second World War the old MFV had been commandeered by the Germans and used in various capacities including salvage and coastal fishing. Oak was mainly used in its construction - the hull was 4 inches thick, and she was one of many hundreds built to fish in the stormy oceans around Sweden and the North Sea.

After satisfying himself that Beth was really the boat he wanted, Don went home and told his wife, "Moylia", Don's pet name for Lena – a corruption of the Italian 'Moglie' meaning wife. "I've bought a boat and we're going to Australia". Her reaction, in Don's words, as he later told the story, was, "Here we go again, I suppose I had better find something to wear." This somewhat lighthearted quote of Lena's is really not that far from the truth. Such was Lena's faith in Don she would have agreed to just about anything he proposed.

There was no opposition from Don's immediate family. They had learned long ago what sort of a man he was. When the going got tough, he tried even harder, and his determination to see any job through was part of his character that was well known to them. Lena and the boys were understandably proud of him, and placed implicit faith in his decisions. They were a team, and what lay ahead of them could not have been accomplished had they not been so.

With a decision on the vessel made, planning of the voyage began in earnest. It was Don's intention to move into Beth as soon as he got her to England. He knew there would be no difficulty in selling his business. The house and contents would take longer, so Lena would have to look after that. Jonathan still had to go to school and Peter would continue with his job as a motor mechanic until much nearer the departure date. With Don working full time on the boat, outgoing finance would exceed incoming, but with the sale of his Volvo truck and trailer, plus the house, he calculated he could fit out the boat over a period of up to a year, plus make the voyage - say, six to nine months, and have sufficient money left to start off in Australia. Beth was going to cost only £700, a real gift considering some of the boats that Don had looked at.

He listed all the things he would require. First he would get rid of the original Bolinder two cylinder engine and fit a more modern and reliable diesel. The mast was rotten and would have to be replaced. Beth required sails. The radio would have to be overhauled. The decking had to be replaced in some areas. There was no toilet on board. Don went through the list and was convinced he could make it in the time and within the budget he had allowed. He was happy now that he was really able to do something positive.

For the next three weeks he spent his spare time tracking down the other partner who had joint ownership of Beth with Lars Eric Ellinson, and obtaining his approval to purchase. With agreement from both of the owners, the sale had to be completed through a solicitor. There was a lot to be done - he hadn't realized that the transaction could be almost as protracted as a house purchase, and without the help of his French friends it would have been almost impossible.

When he started negotiations for the purchase of Beth, Don had not given much thought to where he was going to moor her. Now the purchase was almost finalized, the problem became very real. He started looking in earnest, and the more he looked, the more frustrated he became. There were not many moorings for rent that were suitable, or maybe he was not looking in the right places.

Then, one day, shortly before he had arranged to sail Beth over to England, he was talking to some locals in the public house in Southampton, where he used to pick up a lot of his trucking work.

"Why don't you give Dave Etheridge a bell? There's not much goes on around here that he doesn't know about. If he can't help you, nobody can," said one.

Don didn't know Dave Etheridge but he made a note of his telephone number and gave him a call. A meeting was arranged for the next day. Dave was a river ferry skipper and knew the area of Southampton Water very well, including all the available moorings and who owned them. When he heard of Don's purchase of Beth, and the reason behind it, he told him of a mooring that would suit his purpose.

"It belongs to Pat Russell, but don't worry, just moor your boat there when you get it across the channel, and meanwhile I'll arrange it with Pat" he said.

Don accepted the assurances of Dave Etheridge. He now had a place to work on the boat and everything was going smoothly. The purchase of Beth was almost complete and several people were interested in his truck and trailer. The mooring was not a fancy berth, just an old jetty, rotten in places, but ideal for the purpose of refitting Beth.

With the purchase of the trawler needing just one signature to finalize the sale, Don started making preparations to get Beth from Le Havre to Southampton. Lars had offered his help, an offer that was quickly and gratefully accepted. Also four of Don's friends from Cranfield had volunteered their services. First the trawler had to be made ready for sea. It had lain idle for quite some time – almost derelict, and parts of the engine had been taken or were damaged. Most of the copper piping had to be repaired or replaced. Missing parts were improvised and broken components patched up. It was a big two cylinder oil engine, sort of a hybrid two stroke, and very difficult to start. Don had no intention of keeping it, so repairs were strictly confined to getting it running and no more.

A date was set for sailing Beth over to England and Don and his friends arrived in LeHavre, ready to board and get underway. The formalities had been completed with harbour authorities and everything was ready - almost. Before leaving LeHavre, Don had to satisfy the French authorities that the boat carried a radio in working order, a life raft, a set of flares and lifejackets etc. After a cursory inspection the harbour officials were satisfied that all the regulations had been complied with – they were probably eager to see the old MFV leave the harbor, and the crew was now eager to board Beth for the trip to Southampton. The weather, however, had deteriorated rapidly since the five had arrived in Le Havre, and a gale was blowing. After some discussion it was agreed to wait until the weather had improved before making the channel crossing, but after four days with no sign that it would abate, the four friends were getting a bit concerned. Their wives were phoning daily, wondering what had happened to them. Two of them had taken part of their holidays to make the trip and were due back at work. On the fifth day the weather did ease slightly and Don and Lars decided to go. Lars said he had sailed in weather much worse and Don was happy to trust him and go along. The four volunteers however, prudently elected to return to England on the ferry!

At 11am on the fifth morning since their arrival in Le Havre, Don and Lars cast off and headed into La Baie de la Seine, and so to the English Channel. The weather did not improve - in fact, in the channel it got decidedly worse, or so it appeared to Don. Lars, on the other hand, did not seem unduly perturbed, and anyway, they were both too busy nursing the engine, pumping the bilges and looking after the helm to worry too much about the weather. It was Don's first experience of sea time in a small boat and one he was not likely to forget. If he was ever to change his mind about going to Australia by sea, then now would have been the time. When he was not operating the big manual bilge pump on the deck he was coaxing the engine or clearing the upper deck of years of accumulated rubbish. Nausea welled in his throat as Beth wallowed in the heavy sea - seasickness was not something he had allowed for, although Lars had warned him before leaving Le Havre that he would be sick during the crossing. With his characteristic determination, Don fought the nausea with sheer hard work - seasickness was to plague him all through the long voyage to Australia. At 7.00am the following morning they sailed into Southampton Water and at 8.30am Beth was tied up at the mooring Don had arranged with Dave Etheridge.

The next day, with the tide well out, Beth was lying on the mud at the old jetty when the owner of the mooring spotted her.

"What the hell is that?" he asked his foreman.

"That must be the old MFV that Dave was trying to tell me about in the pub the other evening," said the foreman.

Pat Russell sighed dramatically. "Oh no, not another one of Dave's friends. Get it out of here will you." With that he marched off in the opposite direction, muttering darkly about every Tom, Dick and Harry using his property as if they owned it.

The foreman picked his way along the old jetty, taking care not to step on any of the rotten timbers.

"Ahoy there," he called.

Don poked his head through the after hatch - he was covered in black grease, having already started to tidy and clean up around the boat.

"What can I do for you?" he said.

"Are you the owner of this boat?"

"Yes, why?"

"Who gave you permission to use this mooring?"

"Is it yours?"

"No, it belongs to Pat Russell, Marine Services, I'm his foreman. He wants you out of here on the next tide".

"Hang on a minute mate; I've got permission from the owner". Don was indignant.

`Well, you had better come along and tell him that, he doesn't know anything about you".

"Be right with you". Don clambered up to the jetty and followed the foreman to Pat Russell's office.

On arrival at the office, Don introduced himself and explained about the boat and his plans, and how Dave

Etheridge had told him about the arrangement for the mooring.

"Look Mr. Caisley, you're wasting my time and your money. You're not going to Australia in that old tub, now be honest. I've heard that same story from several people who have used the mooring. They all left without paying their bills and not for Australia either".

"I'm serious about this project, Mr. Russell and I've got every intention of paying my way. I've never run out on a debt yet, that's not the way I do things. Can I give you a deposit now?"

After talking to Don for a few minutes, Pat Russell must have seen something of his character and his attitude softened towards him.

"No, I don't want a deposit. If you can give me a banker's reference you can have a monthly account".

Don agreed, he supplied his bank manager's name and telephone number in Bedford and the account was arranged. From then on work proceeded without interruption and a good relationship was established with Pat Russell and his staff.

They followed Don's refit of Beth with interest, providing assistance and technical help and were among the many friends the Caisleys made during the year on Southampton water.

*****

Beth Gets A Facelift

As soon as Don had got Beth to England he called Lena and asked her to come down to look at the boat. Lena drove down with Peter and Jonathan, hardly expecting to see a luxury yacht, but definitely not prepared for Beth.

"Yuk!" was the first word expressed as she climbed the ladder up the old trawler's scruffy hull. Once over the gunwale, her disgust became even more apparent.

"Don, this is horrible. It's not a boat, it's a garbage tip." On further inspection, down into what was once the fish-hold and then to the engine room, and finally to the foc'sle, she made it quite plain to her husband that she did not approve of the purchase - and even less of his idea to go to Australia in such a boat. She climbed the ladder to get back to the upper deck.

"I'll be sick if I spend another minute down there. It's really foul," she said.

"Moylia, aren't you going to look at the bunks?" Don called up from the foc'sle. There was no answer.

Lena walked to the after part of the trawler and stood looking over the stern. She looked at her hands and her clothes, where they had touched the boat.

"Yuk!" she said again.

Don climbed out of the foc'sle and saw Jonathan trying to wipe some grease from his hands.

"Daddy, why is the boat so smelly? Do all boats smell like this?" Jonathan's face was screwed into an expression of total disgust.

"Never mind that, son. Where's your mother?" he asked. Jonathan pointed to the rear of the boat. Don went to his wife and tried to persuade her to go back to the foc'sle.

"Moylia, it's not as bad as all that. Once we get it cleaned up it'll be real cosy. You'll see."

"What do you mean, we get it cleaned up?" Lena stressed the 'we'. "Don, it stinks. Whatever has it been used for?" She folded her arms and did not try to hide her disgust for the boat.

The old trawler had been badly treated. In its time as a salvage vessel, Lars had dragged bits and pieces from the bottom of the sea and thrown them into the hold, without cleaning the slime from them. All the muck and rubbish had accumulated in the bilges and on the bulkheads. The result was a stench, which permeated the entire interior of the hull. Not a normal boat smell of tar and red lead, but a foul stench that defied description.

Don could not hide his disappointment. He had not expected Lena to be overjoyed at seeing Beth, but he had worked so hard at getting the boat and made so many plans for the refit. In his mind's eye he could see Beth, not as a filthy, smelly salvage boat, but as a very comfortable vessel with a wardroom, galley, full set of sails and new decks. In fact, he was so rapt with the refit of Beth and the plans he had made that he was oblivious to the stark reality that the old trawler was filthy and stinking.

"I'm sorry, Moylia. I should have cleaned her up a bit before bringing you down here," he said dejectedly. "The fact is she is a very solid boat. I've looked at a few MFVs, as you know, and I've seen how comfortable they can be made. This is probably the worst example you could see. But it will be OK. I'll make sure it is."

Lena turned to look at Don. She knew how much work he had put into buying Beth, and how much the project meant to him. She also knew that once he put his mind to doing something, he would finish it and make a good job. All through their married life he had been a man of his word - the trouble was he could not always convey to others plans that were in his mind. She had looked at some of the sketches he had drawn just after seeing Beth but had not taken much notice of them. Standing at the stern, she unfolded her arms and her expression softened.

Don noticed the change with a certain amount of relief. When Lena had her arms folded across her bosom it was a very bad sign.

"It's quite a big boat, Don," she said. "But do you think we'll ever get rid of that smell?"

"Of course we will, Moylia!"

"Well, what are we waiting for? Get me some air freshener aerosols and disinfectant and I'll help you clean it up." Lena turned from the stern and walked back to the hatchway leading down to the foc'sle. Don followed, hardly daring to say a word.

For over two hours they sprayed, scrubbed and scraped. Jonathan wandered in and out of the work area, but didn't stay below deck too long. Down in the forward part of the boat the stink was almost overpowering.

"That's enough now, Moylia. Let's leave it for now." Don was beginning to feel sick himself.

"No, if I've got to live on this boat all the way to Australia, I might as well get used to it now as later. Don't just stand there, help me." She went back to work with the aerosol cans, spraying every nook and cranny, while Don scraped the filth from the deck and bulkheads.

For the next few weekends Don and Lena spent most of the time at cleaning the filth from Beth's interior. It was not a pleasant task and they had to take a break every hour or so and walk around the upper deck. The foul stench that erupted as the muck was disturbed caused Don to inwardly question his decision to sail to Australia in the old MFV. He never voiced his thoughts about the squalid condition of the boat - there was no need for him to do so. Lena was particularly vocal and expressed her feelings forcefully as she scraped and scrubbed at the bulkheads. After many hours of hard work, the scrubbing and disinfecting began to have the desired effect - the hull was clean, and with the stench gone, relatively pleasant to work in.

During the first phase of the refit, Don removed the lower decking to enable the inspection of the ballast hold. Beth was ballasted with tons of rock, and it had to be removed in order that the interior of the hull could be inspected and repaired, if necessary.

It was achieved by moving all the ballast up to one end of the boat, so one half could be cleaned and painted with a special preservative paint, then moving all the ballast back to the completed end and doing the same with the other half. The operation took a lot of time and effort; some of the rocks weighed several hundred pounds, but it was a necessary part of the overhaul of the vessel.

Once the ballast hold was completed, a new lower deck was laid. The old decking had had heavy objects thrown onto it and was badly gouged and almost rotten in places from Beth's previous use as a salvage vessel. The new deck ran right from foc'sle to engine-room, and as the living quarters were built, was covered in either parquet flooring or Marley tiles, depending on its use.

The forward part of between decks was completed first, because it was to be the living quarters for Don and others during the fitting out. It was originally the seaman's quarters when the boat was used for the purpose it was built, a North Sea fishing trawler. The forward cabin, or foc'sle, was fitted with four two tiered bunks around a triangular shaped table. The new deck was laid with Marley tiles, which proved to be very durable and hardwearing in service. After the bunks, on the port and starboard sides, lockers were fitted. Also in the foc'sle was a coke burning stove, bookcases and a fire extinguisher. Immediately forward of the foc'sle mess, but not part of it, was the chain locker that housed the anchor chain. A door was cut into the after bulkhead of the foc'sle, which led to the galley on the port side.

Behind the foc'sle bulkhead was the original fish hold, which was converted into a comfortable wardroom, where meals would be eaten and the crew could relax.

From a companion way, three or four steps led down to
the wardroom, in which was fitted a table and seating for
eight crew, a serving hatch from the galley, a gas heater,
domestic radio and television set, a record player and

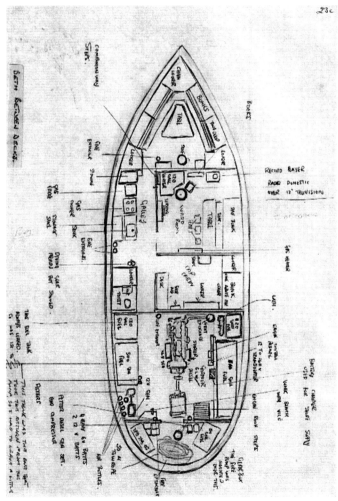

Beth between decks, as sketched by Don

bookcase. The main mast ran down through the wardroom and there was also a 120-gallon fresh water tank in the area. The deck was fitted with parquet wood blocks and the bulkheads were paneled with timber. On the starboard deck head, a skylight was fitted and amidships a greenhouse arrangement of Perspex in frames provided daylight for the wardroom and galley. Above the skylight, on the upper deck, was built a combing that could be battened down with boards and a tarpaulin in case of rough weather. The ability to be able to batten down the skylight was required by the marine surveyor before a seaworthiness certificate could be granted.

Immediately after the wardroom was the captain's cabin. Don and Lena would sleep there and it was fitted with bunks, one above the other on the starboard bulkhead. Two large lockers, a first aid cabinet, a wash hand basin and a desk completed the furniture in the captain's cabin. The entrance was from the companionway on the port side. Adjacent to the wardroom on the port side, Don built a galley containing a gas cooker, a gas refrigerator - which would not work at sea or in any other condition except dead calm, a sink and a drainer, plus all the necessary cupboards and lockers for food stowage and crockery etc. After the galley and opposite the captains cabin was a large locker intended for general stowage and diving equipment. Immediately after that, a toilet with washbasin completed the living quarters.

It was while fitting the toilet that Don discovered just how solid the hull was. There was no toilet on Beth when it was purchased, and Don bought a proper marine unit, using a seawater flush. It had to be fitted with an outlet pipe to the sea in which was incorporated a non-return valve, so as not to allow seawater back into the boat. The skin fitting - a pipe threaded at both ends, with flanges that screwed onto the pipe to tighten up on the hull, and

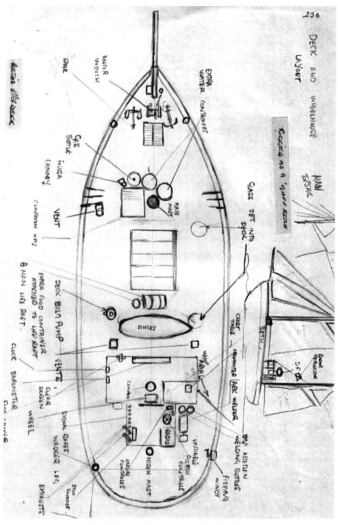

Beth Upper Deck, as sketched by Don

so a large hole had to be drilled to take the pipe. He discovered that he had to drill through four inches of solid oak, which increased his confidence in the seaworthiness of Beth.

The upper deck of the boat was sound, but the main mast was rotten about halfway up its 30ft. length. When Don first looked at Beth, he saw the damage and realised the mast would have to be replaced - what he wasn't aware of was the cost of a proper marine mast. Marine masts are mainly for yachts, and yachts are very expensive boats. Very few mast manufacturers cater for old MFVs, so he had to do some research. Beth did not need a fancy aluminium mast or a high tech carbon fiber reinforced yacht mast - such a mast would cost more than Beth did.

Don discovered a company engaged in making telegraph poles not far from Hythe, at Marchwood, and he went to visit them to see if they had anything suitable. A pole was available, not suitable for telegraph work, but when machined down, would be ideal for the main mast of Beth. The cost of the finished pole was £20, just a fraction of the cost of a marine mast. The telegraph pole mast was as near to the original mast as he had dared to hope for - he was extremely pleased and arranged to have it delivered to the mooring when it was ready.

Meanwhile, the old mast had to be removed. A collapsible scaffolding was rigged around it, and with a chain saw the mast was gradually cut down until only three feet above the deck remained. A square socket was then chiseled into the stump, about four inches deep. The socket would accommodate the custom turned telegraph pole, which was to have a square peg fashioned at the bottom end to mate with the stump of the old mast.

By the time the old mast was down, the new mast had arrived. Don collected a number of hands - there were always plenty of people hanging around the waterfront looking for work or just loafing around, to help him get it on board and step it into the socket of the old mast. It was carried by toggle ropes, along the rotting jetty from where it had been delivered, and onto Beth's upper deck. Unfortunately, one of the hands carrying the mast, trod on a rotten plank in the jetty, falling through and breaking his leg. Don felt bad about it because he carried no insurance to cover that sort of accident. The man was already on National Assistance; being out of work, and apart from visiting him in hospital and taking cigarettes,

Marchwood Jetty – Mast just installed

books and the like, he could do no more. He certainly could not afford to pay him compensation. However, the victim appeared to be far less worried about the accident than Don was, so he took the view that the less said about it, the better it would be, and the matter was never raised again.

The fitting of the new mast continued. It was stepped into the socket previously cut into the original stump and held with a four feet long steel clamp, especially made for the purpose. It was then bolted together with 4 inch steel bolts to secure it. Three steel wires each side of the new mast, were then anchored to a strong point on the side of the boat. A forestay anchored in the bows, a stay running out to the bowsprit; and finally an after stay coming down behind the wheelhouse to the mizzenmast completed the main mast rigging.

With the new mast stepped, the rigging and sails could then be fitted and Douglas Le Ferve - Don's first crewmember, supervised this part of the operation. The rigging and sails were designed as a gaff ketch, with a mainsail, main topsail, foresail and staysail, a gaff sail and gaff-topsail. The sails were designed by Douglas and made to his specification by an old sail maker, in the traditional manner, at a cost of £700 - as much as Don had paid for Beth. When the rigging was completed, Don was extremely pleased with the result - Douglas had done a professional job.

The sails were used throughout the long voyage, but it was not until Beth was well into the Pacific that they were fully understood and used to the maximum advantage.

When Don purchased Beth, he realised that the old engine was obsolete and would be a source of constant worry over the availability of spares and so he intended to replace it with a power unit that was more modern and reliable. But after making enquiries about marine engines - and like the mast, finding the cost too formidable for his lean budget, he called on his own experience with trucks and diesel engines.

An old friend of his, who owned a bus company in Cranfield, had offered him the choice of two engines and gearboxes - a Leyland and a Gardner. Don chose the Gardner because it was slow running and from his own experience, more reliable. The engine and gearbox, in good condition, were still in a double decker bus, which had been involved in a serious accident. They were not difficult to remove from the wreck, but Don found the biggest problem was in getting the engine down to Southampton, once he had got it out of the bus. The only transport available to him was a one-ton van. With the help of friends the engine was loaded into the van and he drove down from Cranfield to Southampton

The old Bolinder Engine bedplate is hauled out

during the night. The weight of the engine had the springs of the van stretched flat, so it was with some relief that he arrived at the mooring without mishap.

The gearbox was transported down to Beth in the same way, but without the worry. It was nowhere near as heavy as the engine. Both engine and gearbox were placed on the deck of the boat, ready for fitting as soon as the old power unit had been removed.

The big two cylinder Bolinder looked as though the boat had been built around it. There was only one way to get it out. It had to be removed piecemeal, pistons, connecting rods, cylinders, valve gear and so on. There was a lot of work involved in stripping it down to its component parts prior to removal. Having dismantled the engine Don then had to find a way to lift each part out of the engine room. A set of sheer legs, using two-inch diameter steel pipe, was rigged on the deck above the engine room, and fitted with a five-ton block and tackle.

As each part was hauled up, it was lowered to the deck and then further lowered to an old landing barge loaned by Pat Russell. Eventually, all that was left of the engine was the crankshaft and bedplate. The crankshaft was too big to be lifted out that way and Don decided to cut it into manageable lengths, with an oxy-acetylene cutter. Not an easy job in the confined space, with the risk of fire always present - the crank itself was almost eight inches in diameter, but after five bottles of gas, the job was done.

Finally, the bedplate for the old engine was all that remained. It also presented a problem, because the after propeller bearing and the variable pitch control gear were attached to it, and they had to be retained. It was not possible to cut the remainder of the plate with oxy-acetylene because of fire danger and the fact that it was made of malleable iron, so Don drilled a series of quarter inch holes across the plate, rather like the perforations around a postage stamp. The holes were drilled so that each hole ran into the other in a line, along which he hoped it would break. The boat was then towed over to Southampton docks where a crane lifted the plate out of the engine room. At the stage where the crane was employed, although the holes had been drilled right across the bedplate, the cut was not fully parted. Don was a little worried that the plate would buckle instead of breaking at the holes. When the crane started lifting, there was an anxious moment before the bedplate finally separated along the line with a jolt, and was then removed. The engine and gearbox were sitting on the upper deck and as soon as the old bedplate had been lifted out, the crane lowered them into the engine room. Beth was then towed back to her old mooring at Hythe.

The whole operation of lifting out the bedplate and dropping in the replacement engine had taken a full day. The removal of the original Bolinder had taken three weeks, but with the job completed, the fitting out of the engine room proceeded without the need to move the boat again until she was ready for the sea.

Prior to fitting the Gardner engine, Don had cut the propeller shaft as clean as possible with the oxy-acetylene, and then ground it flat at the end with a hand grinder. A special coupling had been fabricated to mate the end of the original propeller shaft to the final drive of the bus engine and gearbox. The gear ratios to give best results with the combination of engine, gearbox and propeller had all been worked out beforehand, of course. The propeller's optimum rpm was 300 and the engine's was 1000. First gear was selected because it would give that ratio of engine to propeller speed, and that was eventually fixed. Several other engine speeds and higher gear ratios were tried but it was found that the engine would not successfully drive the big propeller at a higher speed. The propeller was the original two bladed, variable pitch propeller installed when the boat was built, and was almost six feet in diameter. At 300rpm in still water, it would push the old trawler at a little over 8 knots - a speed that was entirely adequate for the purpose that Don intended to use her.

The engine from a double decker bus is gently lowered in position

With the removal of the original engine and the installation of the bus engine and gearbox, the remainder of the engine room was fitted out. The original fuel tanks were retained and several more added - the old engine also had lubricating oil tanks and these were converted to additional fuel tanks. The 6LW Gardner bus engine had a fresh water-cooling system which was not suitable in the boat - it had to be converted to seawater cooling. Don approached the engine manufacturers for assistance or advice in designing a conversion - he had seen similar Gardner engines in boats, and thought a conversion kit would be available. However, the engine manufacturers were not willing to help and showed no interest in the project.

Although annoyed with Gardner Company, he did not let the set back upset his plans - he designed his own closed circuit system, using a heat exchanger to extract the heat from the fresh water and pass it into the circulating seawater. The efficiency of this system was established throughout the year long voyage, as it proved to be reliable and trouble free.

The engine room was fitted with a workbench and vice, and a lathe on the port side. A Petter diesel l2volt generator set and compressor on the starboard side, and a battery charger - adaptable to any shore voltages that would be encountered, was located by the engine control panel, also on the starboard side. On the engine itself was mounted a 24volt generator - to charge the batteries while the main engine was running, and of course, the starter motor. The engine was coupled to the old bus five speed gearbox on which was mounted a fire pump. There were three portable fire extinguishers in the engine room, required by the insurers, and for which Don was to be grateful during the voyage. The decking in the engine room was steel plating and behind it were the propeller shaft and variable pitch linkages and control gear. Above the propeller shaft was a small storage area containing batteries, two fifty-gallon fuel tanks, fifty yards of towrope - another legal requirement, plus various odds and ends that accumulate on board a boat.

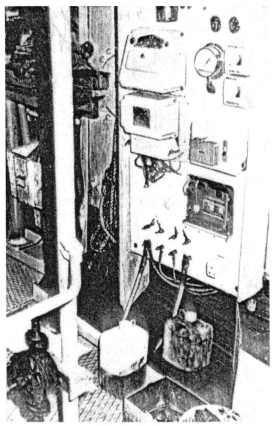

The Engine Room

On the upper deck, starting at the forward end, were the anchor and anchor winch; there was also a spare anchor on the deck. Behind the anchor winch was the skylight above the foc'sle. Next, on the port side, were the companionway steps leading down between decks to the foc'sle, wardroom and galley. Amidships, the mainmast, around which was lashed extra water containers and a gas bottle - used for cooking and heating, and the refrigerator. The chimney from the heater in the foc'sle came through the deck by the companionway steps and a little further aft on the port side, the vent from the galley. Behind the mainmast was the 'greenhouse' arrangement that gave light to the wardroom and galley. Next, the eight-man life raft with an extra food and water container, followed by the dinghy lashed bottom up to the deck. The manual bilge pump was situated on the port side a little forward of the dinghy, and behind that were the port and starboard engine room vents.

The wheelhouse was next and took up the remaining space to the mizzen mast. On the starboard side of the wheelhouse were stowed the oxy-acetylene welding gas bottles and the arc welder. Also on the starboard side was the fishing winch on the gunwale. The Walker log was mounted immediately opposite the fishing winch on the port side.

The wheelhouse itself housed the usual array of marine instruments; at the forward end was the flag looker- situated amidships, the port side of the forward window had a revolving clear screen fitted, a clock and a barometer were mounted on the port bulkhead. The chart table and a chronometer were on the starboard side and the binnacle holding the master compass was centrally located in the wheelhouse with the wheel immediately behind it.

When the old engine was stripped down and removed, Don had thought of selling it if he could find a buyer. Several people along the river had expressed an interest in the old Bolinder, but when it was finally clear of Beth, it was obvious that it was worth nothing but the scrap value. Don sold it to a scrap merchant for a few pounds, but he did keep the exhaust pipe. It was a heavy, solid brass tube, some ten inches in diameter and was ideal for mounting the compass.

The magnetic compass is affected by any ferrous metal in the boats structure that would influence the magnetic field passing the compass needles, either by accentuation or reduction of that field. It was therefore prudent to ensure that the mounting of the compass be as free of magnetic material as possible. Brass, being non ferrous was an ideal choice, which is why the old exhaust pipe was used. It was cut to length and flanged out to take the compass at one end, and mount to the deck at the other. The whole compass mounting was then encased in a polished wood surround to form a very impressive and functional binnacle.

From the wheel, the wheelhouse was only half the width back to the mizzen mast. In that after section were housed the engine controls, the variable pitch propeller control and the ship to shore radio and direction finder on the starboard side. On the port side were the echo sounder and signal flares. The radio and direction finder were part of Beth's equipment when Don purchased her, as was the echo sounder. Unlike the echo sounder which was in good working order, the radio was barely operable - it was purely by chance that Don managed to find a station when the Le Havre harbour authorities inspected Beth prior to her leaving for England – although in hindsight, it probably would have made no difference, so eager were the French authorities to see the last of Beth. Don arranged with the Cranfield College of

Aeronautics - an institution very close to his home and where he knew many of the engineers and technicians, to have the radio equipment completely overhauled and calibrated. The cost of the work was £60 and when the gear was returned on completion a complete set of valves came with it. The radio was fitted with a whip aerial – which was mounted on the side of the wheelhouse, and a direction finding loop mounted on the roof.

The electrical equipment on the boat was powered by 12volts DC, except for the domestic television. All the lighting, domestic and navigation was supplied by batteries, which were kept charged when the main engine was running by the 24volt generator feeding two banks of 12volt cells. There was also an auxiliary power source, a Petter diesel driving a big 12volt generator which was used for charging the batteries when the boat was alongside, or the main engine was not running. Finally, there was a 12volt DC to 230volt AC transvertor which powered the TV and domestic radio. Spare batteries were carried in the after section above the propeller shaft.

Once work had started on the refit, Don quickly realised that, apart from learning about boat building, he also had to become familiar with the language of the sea. The various people he was dealing with - chandlers, sail makers, marine surveyors and so on, all spoke a language that was foreign to him. Port and starboard instead of left and right, mizzen and amidships, freeboard and draught, deck heads and bulkheads. All words and terms that he eventually understood, but that never came easily to his tongue.

From the time Beth was moored in Hythe and Don started working on her, to her departure for Australia, the number of crew and helpers grew. First of all Don advertised in several local papers for a crewman - unpaid of course, but with all meals and board provided. The applicant had to have some experience of the sea and particularly, navigation. Don's knowledge of navigation and seamanship was scant, limited to what had picked up from the Thorenson car ferry captain and crew and by osmosis through his recent association with seafaring people along the waterfront as he worked on Beth. He thought that one extra hand would be enough, provided he had the necessary skills.

There were very few answers to the first advertisement, but one of them, Douglas Le Ferve, was ideal. An agreement was reached and Douglas resigned from his job and moved in with Don, living in the foc'sle. Douglas was to be responsible for navigation.

Another applicant was Brian Goodman - not from the advertisement, but as an old friend of Don from the Northampton Sub-Aqua club. He moved on to Beth with Don and Douglas after he had spent some time on a radio operator's course and obtained his operators ticket. With his newly acquired qualifications, Brian was appointed as Beth's radio operator. Peter, Don's eldest son was the last member of the crew to be signed up. With the four crew members onboard, turns were taken in cooking the evening meal and keeping the living quarters clean and tidy. The foc'sle, which Don had completed first, was extremely comfortable. The oil heater had been removed because of the fumes it gave off, and replaced by a coke burning stove which provided ample heat, even during the winter months.

*****

A Trip To Brixham With A Swash Buckling Swede

About three months after Don had started the refit, Eric Ellinson pulled in behind Beth at the Hythe mooring with a similar MFV called Marga. Apparently he had run foul of the French authorities again, but this time had managed to escape the law by sailing to England. He had put the boat up for sale and had a buyer waiting in Brixham. Eric had sailed her single handed from Le Havre to Hythe - a risky thing to do, but made very necessary by the requirement to get away quickly. The main purpose of the visit was to ask Don if he would help him get Marga to Brixham. The MFV needed at least two crew for safety - especially in coastal waters, and the voyage to Brixham and into the small fishing harbour could not be made safely alone.

Don jumped at the chance, since it would be good experience for him and the other crew members and the opportunity to get some sea time in a vessel similar to Beth was not to be missed. The four members of Beth's crew, Don, Peter, Douglas and Brian would sail with Eric to Brixham and Lena would take the car - an old Morris Minor that Don had bought for running around Southampton, pick them up in Brixham and take them all back to Hythe. Eventually, only Don, Peter and Douglas went with Eric and Lena and Brian went by car.

Marga was in a similar state to Beth – filthy and smelly, and the facilities were Spartan, to put it mildly. Don and the rest of his crew were not too keen to spend a night aboard her and that meant a very early start if they were to make Brixham before nightfall. The tide was also a factor, because the mooring at Hythe left Marga high and dry at low tide, so it was well before dawn and in darkness that they left Hythe.

Halfway down Southampton Water, all the lights on Marga went out. Don and Peter were crawling around between decks with flashlights trying to locate and fix the trouble. They managed to get the navigation lights working by the time Marga had reached Calshot Castle at the end of Southampton Water. The masthead light was still out and as they passed the lightship, a warning was shouted to them that they had no masthead light.

"We're working on it," Eric shouted back and kept going into the Solent. Nothing seemed to worry Eric. He sat up in the wheelhouse smoking what Don has described as the 'foulest smelling pipe he had ever had the misfortune to come across', completely unperturbed that he was sailing into one of the busiest sea lanes in the world, in a boat without proper lights.

As they approached the Solent, the Walker log was paid out so they could measure the distance traveled to help them find Brixham. Marga was a little close as she rounded the buoy into the Solent and the fish from the Walker log fouled the buoy and was lost.

"Don't worry about it," said Eric, "We know the coast."

Don had the local charts and wasn't really worried. After all, Eric was the skipper and Don and his crew were just getting a bit of work experience.

Leaving the Solent and into the English Channel, the sea turned very nasty, changing from choppy to extremely rough. Douglas - who had consistently said he was a lousy sailor, was violently sick. At about the same that Douglas was having trouble with his breakfast there was an almighty crash from the engine room, and all the lights went out again. Don went down to investigate and found the batteries - which had been lashed to the bulkhead with a piece of rotten rope, had broken free. They lay tipped up on the deck, steaming and spilling acid everywhere. The acrid stench did nothing to settle Don's stomach, increasing the nausea he already felt, but he set to work with Peter and cleaned up the acid as best he could. The batteries were re-stowed and lashed properly – no mean feat considering the state they were all in. Douglas was lying down and absolutely no use to anyone. Don and Peter were also being sick while Eric sat up in the wheelhouse, smoking his foul pipe and laughing at them all.

The daylight came and Don and Peter were filthy from crawling around Marga trying to re-stow the batteries and fix the electrics. Eric was a likeable enough character and a good seaman, but the way he treated MFVs – which he professed to have a great love for, was unbelievable. Marga was filthy and stank with the same rancid stench that had given Lena second thoughts when she first steeped aboard Beth.

The old MFV "Marga" can just be seen astern of Beth

No sooner had Don and Peter climbed up from the engine-room when Eric shouted from the wheelhouse.

"Christ! I haven't greased the stern gland. Go and pump a bit of grease in it, will you Don?"

With waves of nausea washing over him, Don climbed back into the bowels of Marga and by this time, he was really suffering. Never before – even on the trip from Le Havre with Beth, had he felt so sick. Everything he touched was filthy and clammy. He found the grease gun but it was empty.

"There's no bloody grease in the gun."

"Well fill it up," shouted Lars. "There's a bucketful down there somewhere."

Brixham Harbour, Devon

Trying to hold back the nausea, Don foraged around the filth and rubbish and eventually found the bucket of grease. Not the sweet smelling, new lubricant that he expected, but a bucketful of a slimy mess that bore little resemblance to grease. It looked like it had been used over and over again, then discarded and sucked out of the bilges to be used again.

He filled the grease gun and his stomach revolted at the slimy mess. By that time the stern gland was squeaking loudly and getting quite warm. Had it been left much longer, it would have broken up. He pumped the mess into the gland until it was full and running quietly.

As he staggered up the engine room steps, he caught a lungful of Eric's evil smelling tobacco smoke, which, on top of his seasickness made him question ever going to sea in the first place. Making his way round to the side of the wheelhouse where he could breathe fresh air, albeit hanging on for dear life - Marga was pitching and bucking like a stallion at a rodeo, he wondered how a man could have the nerve to take a boat to sea in such a condition. What was more of a mystery was how, having got to sea with the boat, he did not seem to have a worry or care in the world.

They rounded Portland Bill and the sea did not get any better.

Eric sat up in the wheelhouse, still polluting the air with his mephitic, tobacco burning monstrosity while Don, Peter and Douglas had their minds on other matters. By then it was getting dark, and no landmarks had been recognized for the past hour or so. Soon it was pitch black and all that could be seen of the shore were lights. Eric got out his 'Book of Lights' to see if he could identify any of them and fix their position and in spite of his sickness, Don was taking mental notes of everything Eric was doing. Up to this point he wasn't too impressed with the Swedish sailor, but he had to admit that for all his devil may care attitude he was a good seaman. His lack of interest over the charts and the Walker log had worried Don at the time, not realizing that Eric had more than charts to navigate by.

Brixham has two lights, one at Berry Head and the other at the main harbour entrance. They had gone past them by the time they had been recognized, so they made a complete about turn and headed for the main harbour entrance. Don didn't know Brixham well, but he knew the inner harbour had a very narrow entrance and was worried about the speed of Marga as she approached. Eric, with his characteristic lack of worry about anything, was through the main entrance and aiming for the small inner harbour, still going full ahead. Although Marga's speed was only around 9 knots, the entrance to the inner harbour was very narrow and it was not possible to see what was inside. Eric did not let little details like that bother him, he was through the narrow entrance and had Marga alongside while Don was still biting his fingernails. When Marga was tied up and secure, Don revised his

Brixham Harbour, Devon showing the town in the background

opinion of Eric up another couple of notches for boat handling.

As they stepped ashore, Don felt like prostrating himself and kissing the concrete jetty. He had never been more relieved to step on solid dry ground before, or since. Peter and Douglas felt the same way. They had arrived in Brixham with barely enough fuel left to go another mile! The three of them, legs still wobbly and trembling from the experience of the past few hours, made their way to the old Morris Minor waiting for them at the end of the jetty. With five of them in the small car, it was very cramped and uncomfortable, but compared to the journey they had just made, the ride back was pure bliss.

As they traveled back to Hythe, Don was making a mental list of the things he was not going to do with Beth. There was no doubt that Eric was a good seaman and could handle the MFV as well as any, and he also seemed to have a sixth sense as far as direction was concerned. What had frightened Don was his complete disregard for the most basic safety rules; the battery stowage, navigation and masthead lights, lack of care over the stern gland and not carrying reserve of fuel. He resolved to do things differently in Beth, but he still retained a sneaking admiration for the swash-buckling Swede, Eric, although he would never go to sea with him again.

With the engine room almost completed and the living quarters finished, Don was making trial runs down Southampton water with Beth, to give the engine a complete work out and generally familiarise himself and the crew with the handling of the boat. After several runs around the Isle of Wight and back up the Southampton Water to Hythe, he felt confident enough to invite his bank manager to spend a weekend on Beth. The bank manager was a friend of long standing and had shown great interest in the project from the beginning.

The invitation was made and accepted, and he arrived in Hythe with his wife one Friday evening. That night they slept onboard, and the following morning, when the tide was right Don prepared to reverse Beth out of her mooring and into the main river way.

Beth gets her bottom cleaned in Marchwood. Lena is in the foreground

The mooring at Hythe was once the departure point for Imperial Airways, which provided flying boat services around the world - before the Second World War, and had been sadly neglected. Consequently the channels were well silted up and only a narrow channel was useable to Don, when the tide was right. It meant that every time he wanted to move Beth from her mooring, he had the tricky job of reversing her through the narrow channel and into the main waterway. On this particular occasion, he ran her aground. The very person he wanted to impress was a witness to his amateurish boat handling and seamanship - however, undeterred he sent Peter over to Pat Russell's yard in the dinghy for assistance, and soon a tug belonging to Pat was pulling him off the mud, and the trip continued. It was a pleasant day out, with the bank manager and his wife enjoying themselves and Don gaining a little more experience of handling Beth.

Scapa Short Solent over the Hythe mooring, circa 1936

His lack of expertise provided entertainment for a lot of experienced people on the river, but it was all good natured, and as each day passed he was a step nearer to achieving his goal. On another occasion, just prior to leaving England, Don had taken Beth over to

Southampton to complete the provisioning for the voyage. The water tanks were filled, the fuel oil tanks were topped up and all the food and stores had been taken aboard. Beth was much heavier than she had ever been. Leaving Southampton for Husbands yard at Marchwood - the place where the final slipping of Beth was carried out for caulking the hull prior to departure, once again he put Beth on a mud bank. He had sailed Beth over the area several times during the past two months - on engine trials, and had never bothered to look at the local charts. Familiarity with the area had resulted in negligence in taking the proper precautions - it was not until Don had left Marchwood on the first leg of the voyage that he looked at the local charts and realised his mistake. Beth was stuck firmly on the mud bank and it would be almost two hours before the tide was high enough to float her off. Don felt foolish as he sat there while other boats passed them, using the safe channel, with the crews laughing and making fun of their predicament - they were in no real danger. Beth was well and truly stuck on the mud, and Don was resigned to wait for the next tide when he was hailed by the skipper of a passing tug.

"Start your engine and put it in reverse," the tug skipper shouted across. "I'll come as close as I can and put some water under you." Don ran up the engine and put the propeller control astern. The tug came at them like a train, making an enormous bow wave that put enough water under Beth to lift her off the mud. With the engines running astern, she backed off the mud and into the safe channel. Grateful but embarrassed, Don took Beth back to Marchwood: another lesson learned - never take anything for granted as far as the sea is concerned!

David Etheridge and friend, picture taken 2004
Courtesy of Dave Etheridge

With the rebuilding of Beth now complete and to Don's satisfaction, there remained only the final slipping of the boat for caulking and the setting of the compass. The slipping was a fairly straightforward job and was carried out at Marchwood - a little way up the river from Pat Russell's mooring. The adjustment of the compass was much more involved: compass setting - like roof thatching, is a dying art and there are few people left in this highly specialized profession. Don had applied to the Southampton Waterways Authority to have his compass set. A time was arranged for the work to be done and Beth had to be at a particular jetty in Southampton to pick up the man from F. Smith & Son who was to carry out the adjustment. Dave Etheridge had offered to go along with Don for the setting - an offer that he was extremely grateful for. Dave had experience of the procedure and could handle Beth well

- there was to be quite a lot of manoeuvring during the compass setting.

At the appointed time and place, Beth picked up the man who was to do the job, who turned out to be a rather elderly man who had to be helped on board. Once on board however, he was the master of his trade and gave instructions to Dave as to where he wanted Beth. The next thing he did was to walk around her, taking note of all the metal equipment on board. He told Don that once the compass had been set, the large metal objects would have to remain in the positions they were at the time of the setting. The arc welder and the oxy-acetylene gas bottles particularly would have to stay in the same position. Don had been warned about conditions and placement of metal equipment and was quite prepared - everything was in its final position.

Looking ship shape just prior to compass setting

Dave was then instructed to take Beth out into Southampton Water to a predetermined spot, and the setter put up his flags to warn shipping to keep clear while Beth's compass was being adjusted. The rest of the procedure was to point Beth's bows in various directions while the setter placed little correcting magnets around the compass binnacle and made notes on his charts. When the job was done he handed Don a complete chart with all the compass points and the necessary corrections.

"These corrections only apply to the Northern Hemisphere. Once you get south of the equator, you should endeavor to have the compass set again," were his final words to Don as he was taken back to the jetty.

Don was never able to find anybody to set the compass in the Southern Hemisphere. To an experienced navigator, the fact that a compass adjuster was not available would have been no problem at all. It is the navigator's responsibility to check the accuracy of the compass, and find out what deviation the boat carries in order to compensate for it during navigation. Where a professional compass adjuster is not available, that correction is made by a procedure known as 'swinging the compass'.

It involves lining up objects that have been identified on the charts, and with the boat securely moored, checking the compass bearing of the objects then pulling the boat around so the bow lines up with due north. With the original variations to the compass applied, the accuracy of the compass can be established, and new variations calculated.

A crash course in navigation would barely have covered the basic use of the sextant in celestial observations: it certainly would not have covered the intricacies of compass swinging and correction.

There was so much to do in preparing for a voyage that was to take the family halfway around the world. Basic requirements like food and water and the technicalities of the trawler itself, had all been taken care of. For rank amateurs, such a voyage was a daunting project, not to be undertaken by the faint hearted, but the Caisleys were made of sterner stuff! 'You can do anything you want if you put your mind to it', has always been Don's philosophy. 'If you're not an expert, then you have to give a lot more thought to what you are doing, and take a lot more precautions'.

There had been no skimping on supplies and provisions: Beth was equipped with sufficient spares to cope with almost any emergency, including spare blocks for the sails, ropes, almost a complete engine in spares, a complete set of valves for the radio, and a well equipped workshop in the engine room that could cater for drilling, welding or even fabrication of replacement parts. Charts, almanacs, pilot books, sight reduction tables - the list of navigation equipment carried by Beth would have been approved by the most fastidious of seamen!

There were however, other requirements that would not have been so obvious to a non seafaring person; for instance, medical attention in the event of sickness at sea, and schooling for Jonathan. Don sought the assistance of a local doctor to equip his medicine chest and get the necessary inoculations and vaccinations for the journey. Apart from recommending the drugs and first aid supplies that should be carried, the doctor showed them how to give an injection. They injected each other with the necessary inoculations - under the doctor's supervision, and gained valuable experience from the exercise with nobody fainting or being squeamish.

With regard to Jonathan's schooling during the voyage, Don had sought the help of various senior teachers and the education authorities. A list of books and a curriculum was prepared, so that Jonathan would not miss out on his education. The voyage to Australia would be an education in itself: something that would broaden and enrich his experience far more than he would gain from any text book or classroom, but Don was determined that his basic schooling would not be neglected.

The original crew members - other than the Caisley family, were to leave Beth prior to sailing for one reason or another. Don was especially disappointed to see Douglas go as it was Douglas who had designed the rigging and arranged for the sails to be made, and he was also the only member of the crew to have any knowledge of navigation. Brian opted out just before sailing time, but by that time Don knew a lot more about the best way to go about finding a crew, and it was no trouble to find a couple of hands willing to work their passage to wherever Beth would take them.

With Douglas leaving, Don had to make other arrangements for a navigator: as the crew he had signed on, like himself, had no knowledge or experience of navigation. All the equipment and charts had been obtained locally, the charts and books from Smiths bookshop in Southampton and the sextant from a retired sea captain on the Isle of Wight. The old captain had made Don promise that he would treasure it and take good care of it, as he had done over the past 50 years. Don then had the means but not the knowledge to navigate.

It was quite a dilemma! The boat had been fitted out and provisioned, the family was eager and ready to go, but to sail without a navigator was courting disaster. The choice of a navigator was not as easy as the selection of other crew members. Hands could be found in any port, generally sailors or adventurers looking for a means to get to another country and ready and willing work their passage. But the navigator had to be responsible for Beth's position and destination at all times. Although the captain always has the final word on any shipboard matter it falls to the navigator to plot the course, taking into consideration tides, currents and weather etc. The navigator must be able to obtain a fix on the boat's position using any of the equipment available, including sextant, depth sounder, Walker Log and D.F. radio. So the choice of navigator would not be someone just working their passage between ports, but a person willing to stay for the complete voyage!

Peter was the obvious choice to fill the vacancy, at least Don could be sure that he would stay with them and complete the voyage.

Don and Peter went to the bookshop in Southampton where they bought the charts and almanacs, and enquired where they could get a crash course in navigation. Obligingly, the man who had originally sold them the charts offered to teach Peter how to use the sextant and the basics of navigation. It was with this rudimentary knowledge that Beth left England on the first leg of the voyage. Further tuition was obtained before she crossed the Atlantic.

On leaving England the crew complement was Don and Lena, Peter and Jonathan, Len Platt, a seaman-cum-bus driver who finally joined them in Falmouth, Pat, a young man from a local engineering factory and a student, Tony.

*****

Beth Goes Back To Sea

'Friday 18/5/73 O610hrs. Left Husbands yard at Marchwood.' This was the first entry in the log of a journey that was to end in Fremantle, Western Australia, after one year and some 17,000 miles.

There was an air of excitement and trepidation as Beth moved out into Southampton Water. Visibility was poor, normal for the area, and Don expected the mist to lift around 7.30am. He had made the trip many times during the course of the past few months but now it was the real thing, and they were on their way.

The party the night before had been to celebrate Lena's birthday as well as their departure, and had not finished late, but all the farewells had been said. Don and his family had made a lot of friends on Southampton Water during the past year, and everybody wished them well. Naturally, there were some who had doubts that they would make it - people who knew the sea and its hazards and had spent a lifetime around boats and ships. They did not voice their opinions at the party, but they knew what Don was undertaking was fraught with uncertainty and even danger.

Don, on the other hand, had no misgivings. He had planned and worked hard for more than a year to achieve his goal - Beth had become almost an integral part of him and he knew her intimately. How Beth would respond to this love and care as they sailed the oceans of the world, he was about to find out.

At 7.40am Beth was off Castle Point, visibility was still poor, but clearing, when the first mishap occurred. When Beth left Marchwood she was towing a small dinghy - it was not worth much but Don was loath to get rid of it even though he had another one on board. The sea was a little choppy and the dinghy was getting swamped, so it was decided to haul it inboard. Beth was still making her usual eight knots and rather than stop the engine, Don and Peter tried to haul the dinghy in from the side. Unfortunately, it got caught in the propeller wash and was swamped - the little boat nosed down and was mashed up by the propeller.

About three minutes after this incident, a helicopter hovered overhead - Beth's crew were never certain whether someone had been watching from the shore or if it was just another farewell.

The helicopter hovered close by for a couple of minutes and the Caisleys waved to the crew, who waved back and gave the thumbs up signal and then departed.

An hour or so later Beth was off G.C. cottages and Don set his first course - 243 degrees, for the Solent Bank. By this time the visibility was improving and Lena decided a cup of tea would not be unwelcome. Don was in the wheelhouse with Peter, Jonathan and Pat, the weather was fair, and although the sea was choppy, it was not uncomfortable. Don remembered the cruise to

Brixham with Eric Ellinson along the same course a few months earlier. He was already feeling nausea but did not show or mention it. Lena called to Jonathan to help her with the tea; however, Don had already decided he would rather have a Coca-Cola - he said his stomach was still feeling the effects of the party last night.

Soon they were out of the Solent and past the Needles Lighthouse. Their destination was Weymouth. By 2.15pm they were off Swanage and could see the lighthouse on Durlston Head. Looking ahead they could just make out Portland Bill, and within two hours were alongside in Weymouth. The first stop among many, 58 miles on the Walker log, unsupervised. Don felt pleased with himself after he had brought Beth alongside and tied up.

"I'll have that cup of .tea now, Moylia." he said, as he came out of the wheelhouse.

The next four days were spent shopping and looking around the seaside resort. Don had promised his family that he would make it up to them for the years he had spent away from home and the voyage to Australia would be a holiday cruise. No rushing to meet deadlines or keep appointments, just a leisurely cruise, going where they wanted to go and staying for as long as they wanted. This first port of call was to set the pattern for the rest of the journey.

Weymouth, an ancient town with a safe harbour, owes its popularity as a resort to George III, who first bathed in the waters of Weymouth Bay in 1789. Following the monarch's example, hundreds of wealthy Georgians descended on the town and the results could be seen as the Caisleys walked along the Esplanade, in the many examples of Georgian architecture.

Up until now, Don had never really shown much interest in the history or origins of places. Most people take for granted the towns and villages of their homeland, knowing only a few of the more popular historic moments associated with them. This was the beginning of a voyage that would take Don and his family halfway around the world, and visit many ancient and history steeped places. It was an added pleasure to learn a little about the areas they were traveling through. On a visit to the Isle of Portland, which shelters Weymouth harbour, they saw the quarries where the famous 'Portland Stone' comes from. This superb limestone has been used in many famous buildings worldwide, two of which are St. Pauls Cathedral in London and the United Nations Headquarters in New York.

While in Weymouth, Don took on 52 gallons of fuel and topped up the tanks with fresh water - Beth carried enough fuel for 3500 miles, but ever cautious, he was to fill his tanks wherever possible. The memory of the trip to Brixham with Eric Ellinson – arriving with empty fuel tanks, was still fresh in Don's mind.

On Wednesday 23rd. of May at 11.15am they pulled away from the jetty at Weymouth, bound for Brixham. The sea had a medium to heavy swell and the wind was from the west. Out past Portland Bill a course was set for 230 degrees, and Beth was behaving as she normally did in a swell, pitching, tossing and rolling. Don was seasick, but not incapable as Beth thumped on. About two hours out of Weymouth, a crash was heard in the engine room and more bad memories of the trip to Brixham with the Swedish sailor flashed across his mind.

Don left the wheelhouse and raced down the engine room steps to investigate. He had visions of batteries tipped over and acid eating into the deck causing acrid, choking fumes, but he tried to force them from his mind. When he got to the source of the crash he was relieved to find the batteries were secure. The workbench in the engine room had three drawers, each of which held an assortment of nuts, bolts and washers and sundry small items. The drawers had broken out of the bench with the violent bucking of the boat and most of the contents had dropped into the bilges under the engine. The bilge pump had sucked some of the spilled items into its relatively delicate interior, wrecking the impeller and the next few hours were spent groping under the engine into the bilges and trying to get the remainder of the hardware out. Unless the bilges were completely cleared, a replacement pump would be wrecked in a similar manner, so it was imperative to make sure all the spilled hardware was removed.

It was 8.00pm in the evening when Don dropped the anchor in the outer harbour of Brixham, after almost nine hours of buffeting in the heavy seas. With the anchor secured, Beth rocked lazily in the shelter of the harbour with the wavelets slurping at her hull - the past nine hours just a memory. With the pounding engine now silent, the crew started coming to life. Seagulls swooped and shrieked overhead as if welcoming Beth to this picturesque fishing port and everybody on board was happy to see the harbour. Jonathan, who had started keeping a diary, recorded: '*On the way to Brixham I was sick three times, Mum as well. When we got there we were very shattered.*'

It says much for the Caisley family that the first experience of bad weather did not deter them from continuing: everybody on board was sick and Lena could not swim - Don's determination had obviously rubbed off on the rest of the family. If there had been any misgivings about the voyage, surely this would have been the time to voice them.

Brixham is a delightfully quaint fishing village in the south of Devon. The major residential part is built on a hill, looking down over the small fishing harbour. It was an ideal spot to relax, and that was what the Caisley family did for the next few days. They stayed anchored in the outer harbour, so no fuel or water was taken aboard, but Don was kept busy in fitting the new bilge pump and in arranging a more secure stowage for the drawers and other moveable objects in the engine room and around the boat generally.

After a pleasant and relaxing stay in Brixham, they were ready to face the sea again. Don, doing everything according to the book, informed the local harbormaster of his intended destination and estimated time of arrival. The log recorded: 0515hrs 'up anchor', and at 0530hrs 'underway'.

Beth was bound for Falmouth in Cornwall, the last port of call in the Caisley homeland.

The lowering and raising of the anchor was always a protracted affair. The chain locker - which housed the anchor chain, was just forward of the foc'sle, and just dropping the anchor would have had the chain thrashing around in the locker and doing untold damage. Similarly raising the anchor had to be done carefully. The anchor was lowered with the chain being winched down manually by two of the crew, and the chain in the locker being fed out by another crew member, usually Jonathan.

It was raised on the winch - again with two of the crew, and the chain was laid out on the deck as it came inboard. After the anchor was up and stowed, the chain was hosed off and fed back in the locker.

The trip to Falmouth passed without any incident worthy of note, the sea turning magnanimous towards them and providing a smooth passage - as if relenting from the harsh treatment meted out previously. Beth arrived at her destination at 4.30pm after eleven uneventful hours. That first leg of the voyage - from Southampton via Weymouth and Brixham, was more by way of a training cruise than anything else. Don wanted to familiarise himself and his family with life at sea and watch keeping. It was also of vital importance that Beth be put through her paces, and so that in the event that any problems occurred, they could be rectified in familiar surroundings.

Don went ashore and saw the harbormaster - which was the correct procedure. He was told that the newspaper reporters had all been waiting for them in Plymouth, and had raised an alert thinking they had been lost at sea. Where the misunderstanding had been made, Don was never sure, or really cared. He had given his destination and estimated time of arrival to the harbormaster in Brixham who had relayed it to Falmouth, where they were expected. The media people had not got their facts right – they appeared to be more interested in sensational headlines and supposition, so why should he worry. The people that mattered had the correct information. Understandably, Don was not impressed by the reporters he had seen so far. They had been extremely critical of his venture and had harassed himself and other members of the crew on several occasions.

With what appeared to be a safe anchorage in Falmouth, everyone went ashore – it was the first and only time that Beth was ever left completely unattended. While they were all ashore, a stiff breeze blew up and caused her to drag her anchor. Don saw it happening but from the shore could do nothing. The anchor did not drag far, but got caught in other anchor chains that were holding down some large pontoons. He hurried back to Beth and once onboard, tried to raise the anchor in order to move the boat to a safer position. The anchor was well and truly caught, and the only way to free it was to cut the chain. With the chain secured - so it could not slip over the side as soon as it was parted, Don cut through. He then tied a large plastic container to the cut end of the chain and let it go over the side. Beth was then moved to a safer anchorage and secured using the spare anchor. With the boat securely moored, Don put on his diving gear and went down to retrieve the fouled anchor and chain. The harbormaster later commented on his thoughtfulness in salvaging the anchor and chain - he said most people would have left it where it was and not have bothered, leaving it as a hazard for other boat owners. To Don it was more a matter of economics than anything else - anchors and chain cost money!

After the incident with the anchor dragging, a deck watch was kept on Beth any time she was in port. The next few days would be spent sightseeing and, for Don, preparing Beth for her voyage to Portugal.

During the age of sail, Falmouth - the southernmost port in England, was a regular stop for merchantmen coming from Europe, Africa and America. Messengers and ambassadors would be dropped off in Falmouth because it was quicker to travel overland by stagecoach or on horseback, than a ship could tack against the wind up the English Channel. Henry VIII, aware of the strategic position of Falmouth at the entrance of Carrick Roads, built Pendennis and St. Mawes castles, facing each other across the roads. Later, the port became the

To Australia – with 'Beth' and a bus engine

GRAHAM STANFORD meets the man who packs up his Cranfield truck business and embarks with his family on a new life in a 58-foot boat he bought and renovated.

Don Caisley with his mother and wife aboard Beth.

communications centre of the British Empire, with the first Royal Mail packet station being centered there.

Falmouth is now one of the leading resorts on the Cornish Riviera, and Don, Lena and the boys found plenty to see and do. The climate is unlike anything else in the British Isles - one doctor extolling the virtues of the Cornish weather said the winter there was just like a sluggish spring. Certainly subtropical plants and trees grow there without special attention and even olive trees bear fruit.

Don had a good selection of chandlers and ships provisioners to choose from, some of the establishments dating back to the days of sail. As he was leaving England, he also made all his duty-free purchases there, including a .303 rifle and ammunition. It was a big surprise to him to find that firearms can be purchased by anyone, without a permit, in England. Production of the ships papers was all that was necessary.

Just prior to departure from Falmouth, the newspaper reporters located Beth and began their usual line of 'inexperienced people going to sea, creating problems for others and being a menace to shipping'. By this time Don was thoroughly fed up with the press. They had nothing constructive to say and generally tried to belittle him, he thought. One reporter came out to Beth in a small boat, but Don would not allow him aboard. His stance was vindicated a year later, when the Caisley family's safe arrival in Fremantle, proved the media pundits wrong.

On Tuesday, June 5th Don went to see the harbormaster and gave him details of the next leg of the voyage. The destination was Oporto in Portugal.

"What do you feel about leaving England?" he was asked by a small group of people as he prepared to cast off.

"I've got no feelings about leaving, no lump in my throat and no tears in my eyes. I'm leaving with no regrets whatsoever." he answered to their surprise. He could have added his heart-felt thoughts about England and the Common Market, but that would have only delayed him, and not served any useful purpose.

At lunchtime, Beth slipped quietly out of Falmouth. The wind was from the north east and Don set the sails and put the walker log out. A course was set for 170 degrees, and once clear of the English Channel and into the North Atlantic, the course was changed to 230degrees.

Soon they were out of sight of land and getting further into the North Atlantic with every revolution of Beth's big propeller - no longer could they rely on landmarks to navigate by. Peter's hastily acquired navigational skills had now assumed paramount importance.

The practice sightings he had made up to then had mainly been while standing on solid ground. To take a sextant sighting from the heaving deck of Beth was a different matter: Peter was confident that he could make an observation, and calculate their position with his limited training as he waited for the sun to break through the clouds. Several times he went to the wheelhouse and carefully took the sextant out of its case. Holding it this way and that, he inspected the delicate instrument, checking the cleanliness of the mirrors and lens. Pointing it at the horizon he peered into the eye-piece, as if inviting the sun to appear and be sighted.

On the first day out from Falmouth, the sun remained hidden by a heavy cloud cover and the sextant could not be used. In fact, for the next four days it took to reach Portugal the sun was not sighted. It was a big disappointment to Peter not to be able to use the sextant, but he was still responsible for navigation. If a celestial sighting could not be taken, then the piloting would have to be done by dead reckoning. With the captain, he applied all the data to hand in plotting Beth's progress. The speed, course, time, wind and currents were calculated against the reading on the Walker Log. The echo sounder and DF radio would be used as they approached nearer to land.

After 168 miles, the automatic bilge pump that Don had purchased and fitted in Brixham, ceased to function. Not a big problem - it just meant switching to the main circulating pump for bilge clearing, but it was annoying. After 295 miles, a fuel blockage to the main engine developed and was quickly cleared, and at 453 miles out from Falmouth, a block on the main sail broke - Don had been warned that the wooden blocks were prone to shattering by continually banging against the mast, and so he had included several spares in his provisioning for the voyage. The sail was hauled down and stowed so that the block could be repaired or replaced in harbour. On the 9th of June, at mid-day their position was confirmed by a DF sighting, Beth was off Cape Finisterre and sailing parallel to the Spanish coast. The weather was then getting very foggy and soon the fog had closed in and visibility was down to 200yds and so Don was sounding the hooter every two minutes to make Beth's presence known to other shipping in the area. She carried no radar and although most other shipping would have been so equipped, Don, ever cautious preferred to be safe rather than sorry.

According to the dead reckoning calculations that Peter had made during the past few days, they should then have been approaching Oporto.

The echo sounder was switched on and it showed that the seabed was rising. As the fog began to clear, land was sighted, and peering through the mist Don could just make out a lighthouse on a headland. The pilot book was consulted – it contained a section showing silhouettes of prominent landmarks and it confirmed that the lighthouse they had seen was in fact, Lecca Lighthouse. At 3pm that afternoon, Don dropped anchor in Lexioes – which is the seaport serving Oporto.

They had come 617 miles and made their first foreign landfall, within 5 miles of where they intended. Sailing through fairly heavy seas and fog, with no chance to use the sextant, relying only on the Walker log, the DF radio and the echo sounder, Peter felt quite pleased with himself. Don was also relieved as he congratulated Peter, but made no mention of it. To a seafaring person, that landfall would have been no achievement at all, but the Caisleys were rank amateurs with no experience whatsoever. Don recalls they felt a bit like sailors by then!

The correct procedure on entering a foreign port is to raise the yellow quarantine flag and wait for the arrival of the customs officer, and this was done once Beth was anchored in Leixoes. The first person to come aboard however was not a customs officer, but a padre from the Flying Angel missions to seamen.

"You will have to go and see the customs officers. They'll never come out to you," the padre told Don after the usual pleasantries. This was quite a surprise to Don, but undaunted he went ashore and presented the boats papers to the customs officials. They were given a clean bill of health and told they could stay as long as they liked.

The visit from the padre was Don's first encounter with the Flying Angel, and he viewed the padre's visit with a little suspicion at first. His first thoughts were, 'here we go again, you can't even get away from the bible bashers at sea. What with Jehovah's Witnesses and Mormons banging on your doors in England, and now this bloke in Portugal. I suppose we will all have to put up with him preaching a sermon to us before we can get rid of him.'

How wrong he was! The padre was unlike any parson or preacher he had ever met. His main interest was for the welfare and comfort of the crew. He told Don of a swapping library of books he had, and also gave him a list of addresses where he could collect mail throughout the rest of the voyage. If the Caisley's wanted religion, they could have had that too, but it was not a condition for providing assistance. They were agreeably surprised, and in fact, visited the Flying Angel throughout the voyage.

Oporto is situated at the mouth of the Douro River, which is some 485 miles long. Across the dry and dusty plains of Spain, the river flows until it reaches Portugal where the scenery changes. From windswept plains, the river then flows through a narrow rocky valley, and it is on the sides of this valley that that the red-purple grapes are grown from which Portugal's famous port wine is made. Oporto is the centre of the port wine trade and in fact, gave its name to the wine. The Caisley's spent several pleasant days sightseeing, visiting the wine lodge and watching the bustle of shipping trading in and out of Lexioes.

While they were in Lexioes, they were anchored not far from an expensive looking motor yacht or cruiser. Soon after their arrival, the owner sent 'his man' over to Beth to see the captain.

"Would you mind terribly, not visiting us?" was the message he brought. "We are on holiday and trying to make contact with the locals." The inference was that they were high class aristocrats and the Caisleys were working class, and they wanted nothing to do with them. Don and the family were amused by this approach and by the messenger's obvious embarrassment. They had not intended to visit them anyway, but they were friendly towards the servant and he was made welcome - the man made several subsequent social visits to Beth while the Caisleys were in Leixoes. Don was quite prepared to accept that he and his family were not up to the aristocratic standards of the owner of the motor cruiser and let it go at that, until one incident changed his mind.

From the jetty at Lexioes, a ladder goes down to the water so that at low tide, one can get into a boat by climbing down. On this occasion, a party from the cruiser had been ashore and was just returning. Immediately behind them, waiting to use the ladder, were the Caisleys. The owner of the cruiser was the first to go down the ladder to his dinghy waiting at the bottom. His lady friend followed and unfortunately stepped on his fingers. From the foul language and obscenities uttered by this so-called aristocrat – not just in the presence of a lady but actually directed at the female who had dared to step on his hand, it was quite obvious that Don had been wrong in his assessment of who was high class and who was rabble. The language came from the gutter and all the money in the world would not have given that man any class.

The Caisley's spent four days in Leixoes, visiting the Flying Angel in between shopping and sightseeing and enjoyed their stay. Don's only regret was that Coca-Cola was not available in Portugal – he preferred Coca Cola to almost any other drink and was almost an addict. They raised the anchor and sailed out of Lexioes in the afternoon of the 13th June bound for Lisbon.

*****

Fire In The Engine Room

At 6am on the morning of the 14th June, Beth was at the mouth of the Tagus River, after a short run down the coast from Oporto. With the old bus engine making its normal revolutions she should have been traveling in excess of eight knots. The MFV was making no progress at all, and for four hours running against an outgoing tide was barely making headway. Had Don read his pilot book correctly, he would have known that the current in the Tagus runs around eight knots, almost the speed of Beth. He was still learning, but eventually he made it to the yacht pens, where he planned to berth. Local regulations required a pilot to go further up the Tagus River, and Don did not want to get involved in extra formalities or expense for just a short stay. By the time Beth reached the yacht pens it was almost dark and Don was afraid to go in - the entrance was very narrow and he could not see what was inside. He anchored outside and raised the yellow flag, prepared to wait for the customs to come out to him. The night passed and with daylight, they were hailed by a man in a small dinghy.

"Are you coming in or not?" shouted the man.

Don told him they were waiting for clearance from the customs. "You'll wait all day, they'll never come out to you. Tie my dinghy up astern and I'll show you in," said the man.

The entrance to the yacht pens was little more than 30 feet wide and Beth had a 19 foot beam. Don was worried about going through such a narrow opening, in case he hit something. Apparently the self appointed pilot had more confidence in Don's boat handling capability than Don had himself. With Don at the wheel, Beth went through the entrance with no problem at all, but once inside, he found small boats everywhere. He was sure he was going to hit one or more of them, but with more skill than he realised he possessed, he brought Beth to a buoy and secured her like a professional sailor.

Tying up to a buoy was always a difficult procedure with Beth. The man at the wheel was blind once the boat was close to the buoy. The men in the bows had to grab the buoy with the boat hook and relay messages to the wheelhouse. On this occasion all went well, and they were alongside the buoy and tied up as though they had been doing it all their lives.

Don collected the boats papers and the passports and went to see the authorities. The customs office was a long way from where they had berthed, but eventually all the formalities were completed and he prepared for the long walk back.

"Can I give you a lift back to your boat?" asked a stranger as Don came out of the customs office. It was an offer too good to refuse, Beth was berthed several miles away and remembering the long walk from the yacht pens, he gratefully accepted and was taken back to Beth in a customs launch.

Lisbon, a city of around one million inhabitants, is built on and around two hills rising steeply from the Tagus River. The city was mostly destroyed by a devastating earthquake in 1755, but was rebuilt and is now one of the most beautiful in Europe, with its fine white buildings and the many parks and gardens. The Spanish Armada sailed from Lisbon - which has been a major port since the fifteenth century, in its unsuccessful attempt to conquer England.

The Caisleys wandered down the Avenida da Libardade, Lisbon's main street, and through many of the narrow winding streets left untouched by the quake. When the city was rebuilt in the eighteenth century, separate streets were given to each trade. The Rua da Prata - street of silver, and Rua Auroa - Golden Street, is world famous for the shops and establishments associated with the gold and silver industries.

Lisbon, as well as being the capital of Portugal and a major port, is also a great fishing port and Don and his family enjoyed a visit to the markets where the fish was being sold. Women carrying large baskets of fish on their heads and barefooted fishermen with brightly colored stocking caps fascinated Jonathan. On every vertical surface, it seemed, were gaudy and garish posters advertising bullfights.

The white buildings, green grass and trees of the parks and gardens and colorful Latin people, all blended to provide a relaxing and memorable visit. Don was happy that his family were enjoying themselves; it was what he had promised them, a holiday to remember. On the 18th of June they prepared Beth for sea and were ready to leave.

This time Don consulted the pilot book a little more thoroughly than he had prior to arrival in Lisbon. Beth sailed on the outgoing tide at 1.45pm. Once through the narrow yacht pen entrance, they were with the outgoing tidal current and left Lisbon 'like a cork out of a bottle'. Past the lighthouse at Bugio on the port beam, and another lighthouse to starboard at Sao Juliao de Barra, they turned and sailed for Gibraltar on a course of 240 degrees for three miles. After three miles Don changed course to 174 degrees and headed for Cape St. Vincent.

It was on this leg of the journey that two incidents occurred to upset the normal smooth running of the boat. In the first incident, Don was expecting a call from the lookout when Cape St Vincent was sighted. The watches were arranged so that two of the crew were always on duty - one at the helm and one as lookout. The lookout spent all his time on the upper deck ensuring everything was secure and that there was no danger from other ships. It was also his duty to look for landmarks and such, if they were in coastal waters. They had sailed past Cape St.Vincent without informing him. Don - normally a placid man, was angry, had planned to follow the coast around to Gibraltar. After telling the crew on watch what he thought of them, a course change was made towards Gibraltar. Shortly after the incident, Don, who was off watch, went into the galley for something to eat. He found the student, Tony - who was supposed to be on watch, making himself bread and jam sandwiches. Don's annoyance was still simmering after the previous incident when he asked who was at the helm.

"Jonathan," replied Tony.

"And who is on lookout?"

"Nobody"!

If the previous neglectful episode had made Don angry, this latest act of carelessness made him furious. There they were in a busy sea-lane, with a nine year old boy at the helm and no lookout. Tony - who should have known better, in spite of implicit instructions to the contrary, had endangered the lives of all on board for the sake of a slice of bread and jam? On arrival in Gibraltar, he was to leave Beth and be replaced.

Caps Trafalgar was sighted and Beth headed along the Spanish coast and into the Straits of Gibraltar. The stretch of water between Spain and Morocco is only nine miles wide at its narrowest point and is renowned for its changeable weather. As Beth entered the straits, the weather - which had previously been sunny and mild, suddenly closed in with visibility down to less than 300yds. Beth, now at reduced speed, thumped on with the hooter blowing at two minute intervals. Suddenly out of the fog, a ship's horn blasted fear into every member of the crew. The ship, which was not seen, was probably over a mile away, but it had brought home to them the need to be alert at all times.

As they came out of the Straits - which is about 25 miles long, that world famous monolith, the Rock of Gibraltar, could be seen thrusting its peak above the mist to catch the afternoon sun. The stark grandeur of the 'Rock', with the sun illuminating its sheer faces, imprinted its image indelibly on the memories of the Caisley's. Don, who by this time had taken over the helm, turned Beth towards the 'Rock' and by 5.30pm on the 20th of June, they were alongside in the destroyer pens of Gibraltar.

For the third time during the voyage Don raised the yellow flag and waited. This time he had not long to wait. A very surprised Don met an English policeman, complete with helmet and whistle, coming onboard. He was shown down to the wardroom where he chatted to them and explained details of the procedure to be adopted in Gibraltar. After the policeman had gone, Don collected the passports and ships papers and went along to see the harbormaster. He arranged to stay in Gibraltar for about ten days and take on fuel and water and other provisions he required. The welcome the Caisley's received in Gibraltar was extremely gratifying and a childhood dream of Don's, to visit the 'Rock' had been realised.

The city and fortress of Gibraltar stand at the Mediterranean end of the Straits of Gibraltar, and is a mere two and three quarters of a mile across, joined to the Spanish mainland by a narrow sandy neck of land. As a British colony since 1704, it is more British than England itself, and Don, like all Englishmen, had heard stories about Gibraltar from the time he could understand them. HMS Victory - Lord Nelson's flagship, came into Gibraltar with Nelson's body onboard, after the battle of Trafalgar, and some of the seamen who died later of wounds received during that famous battle, are buried there.

The Caisley's spent the next week or so sampling the hospitality of the Gibraltarians. With a population of around 26,000, Gibraltar is no bigger than a small town, and most of the inhabitants are engaged in dockyard work, service establishments or tourism. The facilities of the harbour were excellent and Don decided to make the most of his stay there. The eight man life raft he had onboard was by that time nine months old, and due for inspection in three months. He was not sure where he would be when the inspection became due, but he was certain that wherever Beth was the amenities would not be as good as in Gibraltar. He arranged for its annual test and certification - a prerequisite of the insurance underwriter. The life raft had to be unpacked, checked over, and then repacked and Don wanted to witness the inspection. In the event, he did not get to see the inspection, but was sure it had been performed thoroughly.

It was while in Gibraltar that Don started the visitor's book. Somebody from one of the other boats in the harbour at the time, had asked to sign the visitors book and Don realised his omission. He had no record of all the interesting people that had been on the boat from the time he had bought her until now. That omission was rectified and from Gibraltar they had a record of all visitors. Two of the visitors to Beth were Americans who owned similar vessels. They had flown from the USA to Sweden and purchased the MFVs, and were then sailing them back home, using the same route that Don had planned. Don showed them over Beth and explained all the modifications he had made, especially in the engine room, where they were particularly interested to see the double decker bus engine.

Don, Lena and the boys were charmed by their visit to that unique and delightful place. Gibraltar is just a limestone rock with sheer escarpments, a few flat parts where buildings could be erected, and a safe harbour. The 'Rock' itself is honeycombed with caves and tunnels, most of which are man made and not accessible to the tourist. They house workshops, stores, power stations, vast oil and fresh water tanks and even hospitals. The full secrets of the 'Rock' are known only to a few, but there are many interesting things that the tourist can see and do. Some of the caves are open to the public and Don and his family made a special point to visit them. They also saw the rock apes, which are legendary - the famous Barbary Apes are the only wild monkeys in Europe. The apes - actually a species of tailless monkey called Barbary Macaques, were originally brought over from Morocco about 500 years ago and have inhabited the 'Rock' ever since.

A story has it, that while the apes are on the 'Rock', the British Empire will flourish. Of course, there is no British Empire now as such, being replaced by the Commonwealth of Nations, but Gibraltar holds a strategic position at the entrance to the Mediterranean and is one of the reasons why it will remain in British hands. The British Army has appointed a keeper of the apes to look after their welfare and ensure that the population of apes remains on the 'Rock'.

Another reason why Gibraltar will remain British is because the people of this tiny colony have no wish to be anything other than British. They speak the Queen's English, fly the Union Jack from almost every building and are very proud to be British. They are as British as it is possible to be, although they come from Italy, Minorca, Malta and Portugal, as well as England. One can find fish and chip shops and pubs selling English beer as well as British Bobbies on every street corner, almost. They also have their own mayor and city council.

The Caisleys would have loved to stay much longer but they still had a very long voyage ahead of them. Before leaving, Don purchased an additional 20 fathoms of anchor chain and all the provisions he would need to take Beth across the Atlantic. He intended to visit Casablanca and Las Palmas before making the crossing, but was not sure of the facilities there. He also needed another crew member to replace Tony, the student. As usual there was no shortage of hands looking for work and Don selected a young man, Michael - or Ginger as Don called him, with a mop of red hair that he took a liking to. Not much was known about this new member of the crew, except that his father was a bank manager who had kicked him out before the family got a bad name with his waywardness.

Beth was well prepared for the next leg of the journey and at mid-day on the 30th June, moved out of the destroyer pens in Gibraltar and into the Straits. Casablanca was to be the next port of call, some 200 nautical miles away on the Atlantic coast of Morocco.

In the Straits of Gibraltar, the heavy sea mist peculiar to this stretch of water was once again encountered and they sailed through with the hooter blowing. Soon they were out of the fog, past Tangiers and traveling parallel to the Moroccan coast line. Off Cape Spartel and into the Atlantic Ocean, Don turned southward and headed for Casablanca. During the early hours on the 1st of July they were off Larache, and by 9pm the following evening they arrived at Casablanca.

Proceeding with extreme caution, Don was looking for lights to show him the harbour entrance. Ginger, who was also on watch, was chattering away until Don, trying to concentrate on matching the lights he could see with the lights in the pilot book, yelled at him.

"Ginger, for God's sake shut up!" Ginger's mouth snapped tight and he did not utter another word until Beth was alongside and secured. This was one indication that Don, although trying to demonstrate an air of nonchalance to the job of piloting Beth, was in fact, tensed up to the point where the slightest distraction would trigger an outburst.

Jonathan's diary for 30th June reads: *'Got up about 7 30 and had coffee, egg and toast for breakfast. Did my two hour watch and just near the end, saw some dolphins. For dinner I had some sandwiches and the rest of the crew had stew. After dinner I started to make a castle out of Lego, it is not quite finished yet. Nearly Casablanca now. We are about 20 miles away. 9.00. In Casablanca at last and it is Pete's birthday today. He is 18 years old.'*

Food was never far from Jonathan's thoughts. The day after arrival in Casablanca he wrote: *'We went into the town today. There were a lot of beggars about, and flies. For tea I had roast potatoes, beans and chicken.'*

After Gibraltar, Casablanca was disappointing. Don went along to see the harbormaster and customs and immediately ran into trouble. The authorities wanted to take the firearms that Beth carried and lock then up ashore, however, Don refused, remembering advice given to him by experienced seamen in England, 'never allow your firearms to be taken off the boat'. The Moroccan authorities were adamant, but they had not reckoned on Don's determination - short of taking them by force, the guns would stay where they were. During the altercations with the customs, the family went ashore. They looked at the Kasbah and the bazaars, did a little shopping and generally took in the sights.

While Don was arranging for the purchase of fuel and water, Lena bought some fly netting to put over the wardroom skylight to try and keep out the pestilent flies. Casablanca sounded romantic in stories they had heard and read, but in reality it was a rather dismal and dirty city. The flies were coming at them in clouds and the smell was unbearable.

The whole crew was anxious to leave as quickly as possible, and after a visit to the Flying Angel for mail and a final call on the customs and harbormaster, Beth was made ready to sail.

Up to Casablanca the navigation had been mainly coastal, using land marks and the pilot book. From Morocco it would be very different, they would be sailing across the Atlantic Ocean and well out of sight of land. No longer could they rely on landmarks - Peter's navigational skills were about to be tested!

Don and Peter plotted the course to the Canary Islands. They intended to travel southwards, parallel with the coast to a rise in the seabed marked on their charts as Conception Bank. There they would steer a south westerly course bringing them to Las Palmas.

On the 4th of July, Beth was cast off from the jetty in Casablanca and headed out to sea. What with the problem over the firearms, the smell and the flies, the crew were not leaving with heavy hearts. The weather was good and the sea calm as Beth sailed along the Moroccan coast. Just after lunch the following day, Don switched on the echo sounder looking for Conception Bank. There were several rises and falls in the seabed that were shown by the echo sounder, but none that could be identified as Conception Bank and the view was taken by the captain, that they must have already passed it by the time that the echo sounder was switched on.

At 6pm that evening, without identifying the 'bank', they made their course correction, heading for the island of Fuerteventura, which is the closest island to the African coast in the Canary group. By 6am next morning, the island should have been sighted according to Peter's calculations, but was not, so Don took a DF radio sight on Las Palmas - the bearing showed that they were between the Canaries and the African coast.

Don had intended to approach Las Palmas from the north, but with the error over Conception Bank they would turn below Fuerteventura and approach from the south. They would get to Las Palmas a day later than estimated, but it was of no consequence - there was no hurry, no timetable to keep to, and no deadline to meet. The weather was fine and sunny and the sea calm and docile, a perfect day for a holiday cruise.

Most of the crew were in the wheelhouse - an unusual event, when an explosion rocked the boat and had them all running. The noise had come from the after part of the boat and Don rushed to the top of the ladder leading down to the engine room. He was met by smoke and flames as he leapt down the steps. Once in the engine room, he could see that the fire was in the after storage compartment where the batteries were housed.

Prior to Lloyds insuring Beth, they had insisted that several fire extinguishers be placed at strategic points, especially in the engine room. Don had complied and added a few extra extinguishers, and he was now glad he had taken those precautions. He grabbed the nearest extinguisher and with Peter - who had followed him down the ladder, fought the blaze and had it out in minutes. In the event that the portable fire extinguishers had not been able to contain the fire, there was also a fire pump mounted on the main engine. This was started by another member of the crew while Don and Peter were fighting the fire but fortunately it was not needed.

Jonathan's diary 5.7.73: *'Lovely day today. Got up at 8.00 as usual to do my watch. When my watch was over it started to get quite rough. When we were sitting quiet we heard a big bang in the engine room and Dad shot out of the wheelhouse down into the engine room and saw flames in the brig and shouted FIRE! and everybody rushed down into the engine room to put out the fire which never took long to put out.'*

What had happened? When the blaze was extinguished it was obvious that a one gallon can of engine degreaser that had not been properly stowed, had fallen on to the terminals of the battery and ignited the volatile liquid.

The fire could have been serious, but prompt action and the availability of the many fire fighting appliances aboard had averted a disaster. Beth continued on her way to Las Palmas as Don and Peter cleaned up the mess resulting from the fire. The damage was minor, scorched and slightly charred woodwork and paint burnt off parts of the bulkheads and deck head. Some of the items stowed in the area had suffered a little damage, but nothing serious. Once the area was cleaned up, Don looked around the compartment and offered up a silent prayer, it could have been worse, much worse.

The fire had caught them unawares. The sea had been calm, and everybody had been relaxed, enjoying the cruise. It was not the movement of the sea that had caused the can to fall, but the vibration of the engine, gradually jogging the can towards the edge of the shelf until it overbalanced and fell on to the batteries. While they were in Las Palmas, Don would arrange a more secure stowage in the after compartment and repaint the area damaged by the fire.

*****

Turning Back Is Not
An Option

As Beth approached Las Palmas - a bustling tourist resort, the naked, rugged hills could be seen forming a backdrop to the city, liberally sprinkled with high rise hotels. Don piloted the boat into Puerto de la Luz and tied up to the jetty. The seaport of Las Palmas is named after an incident which is said to have occurred there hundreds of years earlier. The legend has it that a party of sailors who made frequent visits to the island, had built a small chapel there. One night an eerie and mysterious light descended from the mountains and hovered over the chapel before disappearing. It happened on several occasions until the fearful but inquisitive natives got close enough to the chapel to peer through a chink in the wall. They were amazed to see the light, by then at rest above the statue of the Virgin, the aura filling the building with a 'glorious splendor'. From that time the port became known as Puerto de la Luz, or Port of light, the name it bears today.

Las Palmas, at one time a major coal bunkering station for steamers going to South America and South Africa, now provides an important oil bunkering service. The

Canary Islands, or land of the Primavera Eterna – Eternal Spring, once the place where the rich were sent to convalesce after illness, is now a popular resort area, well within reach of the average Englishman's budget. The land of the Eternal Spring - or the Fortunate Isles as they were once known, is a paradise for tourists in the winter after the harsh English climate. Bananas, sugar and other tropical crops are grown year round. For the Caisleys, the break in the voyage would provide a time to relax and prepare for the first major ocean crossing.

Las Palmas was to be the last port on the eastern side of the Atlantic Ocean. Between there and Barbados lay several thousand miles of ocean, and any errors in navigation would be multiplied by the distance they had to sail. This aspect of the voyage worried Don - not because he had lost faith in Peter, but because the weather up to then had left Peter with little practice in his hastily acquired skill with the sextant. Don had made up his mind to take on an experienced navigator in Las Palmas, to ensure a safe crossing of the Atlantic.

Around any sea-port in the world can be found many men - and in these days, women, anxious to take passage to one port or another, or indeed, any port, and it was not difficult to find at least a dozen seamen from which to select a crew member. Don soon found himself inundated with applicants, all eager to join Beth, and all of them expert navigators - if they were to be believed. It soon became apparent to him that the claimed qualifications of the applicants were suspect in the most part, and the general quality of the applicants left much to be desired. One thing they all had in common, they wanted a free passage to America. Not one of the men that applied for the position could convince Don that he possessed sufficient knowledge or experience to be able to pilot Beth across the Atlantic.

A decision had to be made - would Don take on the best of a poor selection of aspiring navigators, turn back, or try to get Peter some more training in Las Palmas? Turning back was not an option even worthy of consideration as far as Don was concerned, nor did he fancy trusting the navigation of Beth to some dockside layabout. The Caisleys were a team, and would see the voyage through as a team. They would find a way to get Peter some more training and experience in the use of the sextant and general navigation.

As Beth came into Las Palmas, Don noticed a converted ferry boat flying British colors. It was not long before he had made the acquaintance of the skipper, a Norwegian, and became friends. The captain told Don he had bought the ferry boat and converted it to use as a cargo boat and was planning to sail it out to the West Indies and run cargo between the islands. It was registered in Britain because that afforded more opportunities and convenience than any other flag in that part of the world. Don showed him over Beth and explained the modifications he had made, which aroused a lot of professional interest in the Norwegian, especially when he noticed that Beth carried welding equipment. Over dinner with the Norwegian skipper the Caisleys discussed their voyage up to then and, because it was weighing heavily on his mind, Don mentioned his nagging worry about navigation. The Norwegian was an experienced sea captain, and very well qualified to instruct Peter - he offered to give him a week of tuition in return for welding and other work on his ship by Don. Some of the additional fuel tanks he had installed had broken loose: Don had the welding equipment to repair and secure them, and the captain had seen enough of Don's labors on Beth to know he was capable of first class work. An agreement was made and Don set to work repairing the fuel tanks while Peter gained much valuable navigational training in the use of the sextant, almanacs and sight reduction tables etc.

Las Palmas is a resort as well as a busy seaport, and Beth's stay there gave the Caisleys a chance of a little more sightseeing and relaxation. Once the agreement had been made with the Norwegian skipper, even Don found he could relax and enjoy the trips ashore. The Caisleys met many yacht owners, some were incredulous and skeptical when they heard of the Caisley's plans, and understandably some were helpful and some not so helpful. Advice came from all quarters but the basic ingredient was one of caution. Most said that it was crazy to contemplate sailing to the West Indies at this time of the year, right bang in the middle of the hurricane season - better to wait in Las Palmas until the autumn. The skeptics said they were crazy to attempt it during any season!

Don had heard all this advice before, and while not dismissing it out of hand, paid less attention to it than he would have a month ago. Beth had come through some big seas on the way to Las Palmas and although it was uncomfortable aboard her in rough weather, he was beginning to have a healthy respect for her seagoing qualities. He discussed his proposed course with his Norwegian friend.

"I wouldn't take too much notice of those guys on their fancy yachts, Don. Most of them are fine weather sailors. The first sign of a bit of bad weather they'll run for a lee shore. You've come this far, you can go the rest of the way. Peter can read the sextant pretty well now; he just needs a little more practice. I've told him when he makes a sighting, to make not one but six or seven, and then take the average of the readings. As far as hurricanes are concerned, don't worry about them. There are always plenty of signs and warnings; you just keep out of the way of them. Instead of going straight for the West Indies from Las Palmas, take a long loop south, almost to the equator, and then approach them from the south - that way you'll stay well clear of bad weather. Keep your eye on the barometer and listen to the radio and if there is any indication of a hurricane, stay south until it is safe to continue."

This was the sort of advice that Don wanted, from a man with considerable seafaring experience. The Caisleys had no deadlines to meet; the southerly detour would be no problem at all. Instead of Barbados, Beth would make the Panama Canal via Trinidad.

Another advantage of this route was that Beth would be skirting the Bermuda Triangle - a region of the Atlantic Ocean between Bermuda, Miami, Florida, and Puerto Rico where many disappearances of ships and planes continue to defy explanation.

Not that Don had given this weird and uncanny area of ocean much thought as he plotted the course with Peter, but he had read many of the strange stories associated with the area.

Stories from as long ago as 1492, when Christopher Columbus, with Nina, Pinta and Santa Maria sailed through the area. The crew reported seeing strange lights in the sky and on the ocean and compasses doing strange things and giving erratic readings.

From the time Christopher Columbus reported the strange events in his log until August 1973 when Beth was in the Caribbean, strange happenings and disappearances were being reported on an almost weekly basis.

But it was not until Wednesday December 5, 1945, when Five Navy Avenger bombers mysteriously vanished while on a routine training mission, that the area attracted world attention. It wasn't just the five Navy Avengers that disappeared, but a rescue plane sent to search for them - six aircraft and 27 men, vanished without a trace!

Even to this day theories abound about the so called "Devil's Triangle"- strange magnetic fields caused by aliens using matter transmitters from their covert, seabed bases, and oceanic flatulence - methane gas from the bottom of the ocean, are a couple of popular theories.

Even the celebrated trance-medium Edgar Cayce had something to say about the area. He claimed to have been a citizen of Atlantis in a former life, and predicted that Atlantis would be found in the area of Bimini, which is at the northern edge of the 'triangle'. He told stories of an advanced civilization, that had developed all the inventions we now take for granted, and "weapons of mass destruction" including a giant Death Ray! According to Cayce it was the death ray machine that destroyed Atlantis.

But whether Cayce is to be taken seriously or not, or in fact any of the "Bermuda Triangle" stories are true, some very strange disappearances have occurred in the area; including several commercial airliners, US military planes and some very large freight ships.

The weather In Las Palmas during Beth's visit was warm and dry. On one occasion, Don had gone ashore with the dinghy and for Lena that meant staying aboard as Beth was anchored about a quarter of a mile offshore at the time. The beach looked inviting, but how was she to get there since she could not swim? It was Ginger who thought of a way to take both Lena and Jonathan ashore. Ginger was a good swimmer and suggested that if Lena really wanted to spend an hour or two on the beach, he could tow her ashore in a lifejacket.

Nine year old Jonathan quickly asserted that he did not want towing - in fact, he could help Ginger to tow his mother. Lena agreed to the scheme and a life jacket was rigged with two tow lines. Lena tied the jacket around herself and got into the water and the two boys took the ends of the lines in their teeth and struck out for the beach pulling Lena behind them.

The water was pleasantly warm and with her towel, cigarettes and lighter sealed in a polythene bag, Lena was enjoying the excursion, although mindful of the depth of water between her and the seabed. After a couple of rest periods during which Lena and Ginger sat on a buoy and had a cigarette, the trio reached the beach.

Several hours later, after they had enjoyed themselves on the sand and in the surf, Don - having completed his business ashore picked them up in the dinghy and took them back to Beth.

Preparing Beth for the next leg of the voyage was undertaken with far more caution than any previous provisioning. Two 40 gallon drums were purchased and filled with fuel. Dozens of plastic one gallon containers were filled with fuel or water, and these were lashed along the upper deck against the gunwales. Two plastic containers fitted nicely between each rib, and the whole perimeter of the upper deck was lined with these containers.

As well as working on the converted ferry boat, Don had also done all the repairs necessary to Beth - fitting new blocks and sheets, maintenance in the engine room, cleaning the fuel filters and greasing and oiling where required, as well as repairing and repainting the damage caused by the fire. There was always plenty to do aboard and he could have spent two or three months just maintaining her, but much of the work could be done at sea.

By the 16th of July they were ready to leave. Don went through the list of stores and provisions he had taken aboard, double checking the fuel and water supplies - there was no margin for error out in the mid-Atlantic. Peter was happy with the tuition he had received from the Norwegian captain, and a lot more confident that his navigation would get them where they wanted to go. The following day they said their farewells to all the friends they had made during their stay in the Canaries and at 1.15pm, cast off and headed into the Atlantic.

All the preparation to cross the Atlantic Ocean had Lena a little mystified. While she had been involved in the planning of the voyage to Australia, she somehow had the notion that Don would follow the coast as far as possible. Crossing a vast ocean like the Atlantic had never entered her head when she agreed to make the voyage with Don; however when she learnt of the route, she accepted it with characteristic stoicism.

Flying Fish
And Chips

The weather was good and the winds favorable to Beth as she left Puerto de la Luz. A course was set for 200 degrees and the sails hoisted. With such good winds in the right direction, Don decided to run on the sails alone. The next landfall was over 3000 miles away, and could be 4000 miles if hurricane weather was encountered and Beth had to make a southerly detour. It was better to conserve fuel and arrive with plenty than to have to worry about whether the fuel would last. The Caisleys were in no hurry, and all the difficulties and problems to date had been resolved quickly and effectively. They were getting their sea legs and enjoying the voyage.

With the advice from the Norwegian skipper, the passage across the Atlantic would take them south past the Cape Verde Islands in a long loop, gradually turning westward just above the equator, and coming up to Trinidad from the south. Don placed more value on the advice given by the Norwegian than any other counsel or opinion he had received in Las Palmas. Several yachting people had said they were mad to go at all because of the hurricanes in the area at that time of the year, but Don was certain he would be able to avoid any severe weather. He intended to take the advice of the Norwegian and stay well south of any forecast hurricane activity.

Sailing without the engine, the auxillary generator had to run to provide a charge for the batteries, and just before midnight on that first day out of Las Palmas, it broke down. Don had just come on watch and he started up the main engine to keep the batteries charged while he fixed the auxillary generator. The problem was not serious, as he discovered after stripping the head off the engine. Previously some brazing had been done on the exhaust, and some of the brazing metal had got into the valve gear and was jamming one of the valves.

After a couple of hours the generator was back together and running. They were 65 miles out from Las Palmas and the generator had just been restarted, when the other crew member on watch reported the mizzen gaff had broken. The mizzen sails were hauled down and they continued to run on the main engine, their course still 200 degrees.

As the dawn broke on the 18th, the early risers and the morning watch keepers found the deck covered in flying fish. These peculiar fish, when alarmed by the approach of an enemy, move so rapidly through the water that they break through the surface, whereupon they spread their pectoral fins and glide - sometimes for long distances depending on the wind. Beth was disturbing them as she trundled through the Atlantic and was now reaping the harvest. The crew had discovered the flying fish were good to eat, and a bountiful supply was being delivered - just like manna from heaven to the old Israelites. The fish were collected and given to Lena, who baked, steamed and boiled them. The crew ate flying fish in every way possible, including pies, cakes and casseroles, and enjoyed them. Don was not too fond of fish but when it came to food, he had the minority vote. Lena was in charge of the catering and cooking and performed culinary miracles in her tiny galley throughout the voyage, never serving the same meal twice in one week.

While Don and Peter were busy with the problems of navigation, Jonathan was amusing himself when he was not watching the sea, with a large bag of marbles and various other toys he had brought aboard, including a good selection of Dinky cars and trucks. While he was below in the wardroom or foc'sle, he could run the cars on the deck and the worst that would happen was for a member of the crew to step on one and maybe swear at him. When he was on the upper deck it was quite a different matter. Every day one or more cars would roll out of reach, and before Jonathan could catch them, they would go through the scuppers and into the Atlantic Ocean. The marbles too, followed the same route. By the time Beth had traveled halfway across the Atlantic all the cars and marbles had gone. Jonathan still found plenty of things to occupy himself with. His schooling took up a fair proportion of the time, and after Gibraltar, Ginger proved to be an excellent tutor. As well as the formal education, his father had tried to involve Jonathan in the day-to-day routine of shipboard life - even allowing him to do a two hour watch during the day. That was of course, under supervision - the incident off the Spanish coast was never far from Don's mind.

A housewife's adventure

By Kevin O'Brien

FOR centuries the lure of the horizon has taken men and women down to the sea in ships.

Many can't explain their call to the sea. Suddenly it comes on strong and they are embarked on an adventure they never dreamt of.

Take 41-year-old Mrs Lena Caisley. Just over a year ago she had never been to sea.

She was happy with marriage, her two sons and the security of an English middle-class home in the country.

Last week Mrs Caisley arrived in Fremantle after 12 months cruising in a 40-year-old former fishing boat.

How did she feel about such an adventure? What made her do it?

"When my husband first mentioned a boat I was terrified," she admits.

"I'd never been to sea and didn't

Though she didn't know it then, her adventure started when Britain entered the European Common Market.

Her husband Don's small transport business suffered as a result.

With his future in England in the balance, the call of the sea reached him in the English countryside with memory of a boat he had seen impounded by the French at Le Havre.

"He bought the boat and my first reaction when I saw it was 'yuck,'" says Mrs Caisley.

It was terrified at first about the idea of sailing to Australia.

"But I thought more about the idea and thought about all the places we would see.

"I had always wanted to travel and here was my big chance.

"I had great faith in my husband. I decided that if anything was to happen it would be best if we were all together.

"The fact that I was to be the only woman on board didn't

"I was used to being lonely. My husband was often away on business and I found I could enjoy my own company.

"My youngest son, Jonathan, was nine when we set out. His headmaster told me he would learn more from the voyage than at school."

The big adventure started on Mrs Caisley's 40th birthday when the old fishing boat Beth slipped out into the Atlantic rollers.

It finished last week on her 41st birthday when Beth slipped into the Fremantle Fishing Boat Harbour.

Mrs Caisley says it was sheer coincidence the voyage started and finished on her birthday.

She learnt the hard way to cope with life in her new home at sea, then learnt to love it.

"None of us were sailors and we didn't really know if the weather was good, bad or indifferent," she says.

"Now we can read the signs and know the weather we are in for.

"I managed to cook for the family and crew every day and got used to standing, sometimes four hours on end and eight off.

Mrs Lena Caisley in the galley of the Beth.

Lena in her galley." Weekend News May 5 1974

By the 19th the mizzen gaff was repaired and back in service and on the 20th the log records ' engine temperature up'. The main circulating pump, which pumped water over the heat-exchanger, was slipping its clutch, and as it was not really necessary to declutch the pump, Don fixed it so it was permanently engaged and it gave no further trouble.

It was about this time that Don decided to stop smoking. The continual seasickness and nausea had taken the enjoyment out of cigarettes for him and he kicked the habit. There is none so intolerant to the smoker as the newly reformed nonsmoker, and Don was no exception - from the time he smoked his last cigarette, there was to be no smoking in the wheelhouse while he was there. The watch keepers had to ensure that at the end of their watch all ashtrays were cleaned and put away, and all evidence of smoking removed - the rules were strictly enforced!

The flying fish were still very much in evidence as they continued across the Atlantic, and every day a few would sacrifice themselves for the Caisley's table. Jonathan was collecting them and keeping a record as they came aboard - he noted in his diary: *'Ju21st. On deck I picked up 13 flying fish. For dinner we had flying fish and chips'.*

One night during the Atlantic crossing, Lena and Pat were on the middle watch. Just after they came on watch, Lena had checked the log and the compass, and Pat had taken his first walk around the upper deck. They both settled down to what was generally accepted as the worst watch of all - the middle or graveyard watch. Nothing untoward or exciting happened until about halfway through the watch when a peculiar noise was heard - Lena was the first to hear it.

At sea there is a multiplicity of sounds, but all fitting into a pattern that one becomes accustomed to. The throb of the engine, the generator, the flap of the sails as each breeze or gust of wind is caught, sheets slapping against the mast, the swish of the wake and the ding-ding of the ship's clock were all sounds that the crew had become accustomed to. The noise Lena heard did not fit any of the usual shipboard sounds - it was an enormous, elongated snort that seemed to come from alongside Beth.

"Did you hear that?" she called to Pat

"What?" asked Pat.

"Listen, there it is again." For a moment they both stood quietly, and then Pat moved a little closer to the wheelhouse.

"What the hell is it?" he asked.

"I don't know, but I don't like it. Look over the side and see if you can see anything." Lena by this time was just a little worried. Pat was even more worried, or perhaps a little scared.

"No bloody fear, whatever's down there can stay, I'm not poking my head over the side. You go and look."

"I can't leave the wheel - you know how upset the skipper gets if we don't keep the watch properly." Lena gripped the wheel a little harder. "You're the lookout and I'm the helmsman. Listen, there it is again." Pat stepped into the wheelhouse and they both stood on tiptoe, peering out of the wheelhouse window to try and catch a glimpse of whatever was making the noise.

"It's right beside us. Just take a quick peek over the side?" she asked.

"I reckon we ought to call the skipper. Whatever it is, it must be big and bloody close." Pat's voice had a distinct edge to it.

"No, don't call him. It doesn't seem to be bothering us." Lena did not want to get Don out of his bunk before it was absolutely necessary - he was due on watch at 4.00am.

For several uncomfortable minutes the snorting continued, with neither Lena nor Pat daring to look over the side. Then it stopped, and to the watch keeper's relief, was not heard again. The general consensus of opinion of the crew, as Lena and Pat told the story over breakfast, was that a large and curious whale had been swimming alongside Beth. Whatever it was, Lena for one was very glad when the watch had finished.

By the 22nd Beth had traveled 731 miles from Las Palmas, and with the fire in the engine room still fresh in his memory, Don made sure that all the crew would be familiar with the location of the extinguishers and other fire fighting equipment. Also, should it be necessary - heaven forbid, they would know how to operate the equipment. On the 25th a fire drill was organized and Jonathan recorded in his diary: *'I had a wash today. Dad had a fire drill and I was the fire'*.

Peter was now getting proficient with the sextant and on the 27th the log records the position as 12" 45' N, 35" 57' W, the Walker log reading was 1519 miles and course 285 degrees. Beth was approximately halfway across the Atlantic and the fuel situation was good - better than Don had dared to hope for. As the fuel was being used and there was room in the tanks, the extra fuel that was being carried in the plastic containers was siphoned into the main fuel tanks. That kept the weight below deck level and added to the stability of Beth.

At midnight on the 28th, the Walker log became fouled by a rope that had broken from the mizzen sail but during the next watch, it had been rectified. The noon sight on the 29th gave their position as 12' 29"N, 43' 19" W - this was the point where a course change had to be made. The Cape Verde Islands were then within radio range and a DF sight confirmed the position. They were then sailing parallel with the equator, the weather was very close and humid, but not all that warm – as the crew had expected.

On the 1st of August Beth was joined by an enormous school of small whales. They were all around the boat - literally hundreds of them, making no attempt to interfere or bump the boat - just playing, leaping and diving, and generally acting the way the Caisley's had seen porpoises behave. These large creatures were certainly not porpoises. Looking down from the deck of Beth, Don could see that they had backs as broad as a shire horse and estimated they ranged in length from 20 to 30 feet. From the description it is probable that they were pilot whales or grampus - killer whales. They stayed with the boat for quite some time, providing entertainment for all onboard. Eventually, either because they were growing tired of swimming at the old MFVs' maximum eight knots, or they had located some new source of amusement, they left. At no time did they make any moves that were in any way threatening to the boat, but Don wondered how they would have fared had Beth been a much smaller craft.

Later that day - the whales having long gone, the propeller struck something that caused a vibration that was felt throughout the boat. Could it have been a whale, or maybe a log or some other piece of debris? Perhaps it was a tooth broken loose from the gearing? Don was not sure what had happened, but the engine was stopped and the propeller knocked out of gear. Then the engine was run up again to check the gears; however everything appeared to be normal. Don then went over the side to have a look at the propeller, but a thorough inspection showed no sign of damage. Whatever it was, had gone and left no apparent damage.

He climbed back aboard and Beth continued on her way.

No group of people - family or otherwise, can live in such confinement without generating some friction. The Caisleys were no exception and from time to time tempers flared over petty incidents. Don tried to run the boat with as much authority as he thought was necessary, however occasionally a minor problem would develop into a full blown row. At one stage Peter almost left the boat after an altercation with his father, and it was at times like this, that Lena would exert her influence to smooth the troubled waters.

Throughout the voyage she worked not only as the ship's cook, catering and preparing meals for the whole crew, but kept normal sea watches with the rest of the crew. As well as these duties she performed her role as wife and mother to her family and acted as mediator in the occasional disputes. If Don was the driving force and determination behind the venture, it was Lena who provided the sustaining power.

A typical day at sea for Lena was:

7 00 am	Get up and prepare breakfast for the forenoon watch keepers.
7.30 am	Clear away and wash up breakfast dishes.
8 00 am	Prepare breakfast for the watch keepers coming off the morning watch.
8.30 am	Clear away and wash up.
9 00 am	Make bread (twice a week).
	Make cakes and biscuits (when necessary).
	Help Jonathan with his diary and school work.
	Prepare lunch.
12 noon	On watch. During watch, check dough in engine room if making bread that day.
4 00 pm.	Off watch.
4.30 pm	Prepare dinner.
6.00pm	Serve dinner (dinner was arranged so that the crew on watch could be relieved for 10 to 15 minutes while they had their meal)
7 00 pm	Clear away and wash up. Clean up galley.
7 30 pm	Make pot of tea or cocoa.
7 45 pm	Take drink to wheelhouse.
8 00 pm	Plan meals for next day.
	Do any clothes mending necessary. Wash family clothes.
	General tidy up.

10 00 pm	Go to bed.
Midnight	On watch.
4.00 am	Off watch.
4 05 am	Go to bed.

Lena's busy schedule did not leave her much time to worry about the fact that she couldn't swim. Every moment of her nineteen hour day was occupied to the limit.

Beth's log: 2nd. August, ' mizzen sail broken' - the mizzen sail gave a lot of problems during the voyage. On the 4th, Don noted in the log that Peter was worried about their position.

During the Atlantic crossing there was an undercurrent of foreboding caused by some uninformed talk in the foc'sle. Peter's navigation was being questioned, and naturally enough Peter had heard the talk and it undermined his own confidence. Hence, the entry in the log when he confided to his father that he was not sure of Beth's position. At no time did Don lose confidence in Peter and he was sure he knew where and how the rumors had started.

Len Platt, the bus driver-cum-seaman, was the worrying type and would get hold of only part of a story and elaborate on it - he had convinced himself and others that they were lost. Had he been in the wheelhouse during the sessions when Don and Peter were plotting the course - and been in possession of all the facts regarding Beth's position, he would probably have felt differently.

Peter need not have worried, as his navigation was good. On the 5th the echo sounder was switched on and showed the bottom rising to 50 fathoms - which confirmed their position as somewhere off the mouth of the River Orinocco. Further confirmation came later in the day when the sea changed color to a dirty green-brown and Beth was sailing through bits of trees, weed and other debris. The River Orinocco was in flood and the rubbish being washed out to sea was what they were sailing through. Jonathan wrote in his diary that he had seen a seagull floating past on a piece of wood - they were obviously getting close to land.

Early on the morning of the 6th land was sighted, and as Beth got closer Don could make out the lights on the oil rigs and the flames as the gas was being burnt off. He reduced speed and waited until it was daylight before approaching any nearer to the coast. At 7.00am their position was confirmed as Galeota Point on the south east corner of Trinidad.

When the voyage was originally planned, Barbados was to be their first landfall across the Atlantic. However, after advice from the Norwegian skipper, Don decided to approach the West Indies from the south instead of the east. That made Trinidad the best landfall, and Port of Spain the place to stay. Don then had to decide how best to approach Port of Spain - he could take Beth around the eastern side of Trinidad, over the top and in through a narrow channel known as The Dragon's Mouth, or he could go between the coast of Venezuela and the south side of Trinidad, through the Serpent's Mouth. The northerly approach was the longest, and the southerly route had the risk of grounding Beth in the Serpent's mouth, which is a stretch of very shallow water. The options were discussed and it was decided, as the weather was fine and the sea calm, they would try the

Serpent's Mouth, running steady with the echo sounder on.

Late in the afternoon on the 6th, Beth entered the shallow channel. The water was glassy smooth and Don looked at the shores on either side of him with some pride. Venezuela was to his left and Trinidad to his right. Having just sailed his boat across the Atlantic Ocean, he should have been thinking in nautical terms. The satisfaction he felt as he and his family sailed into the waters of the West Indies was in no way marred by his use of non-nautical terms. As a truck driver, 'left hand down' meant more than 'hard a' port.

"How much water have we got, Peter?" Don called from the helm. The bottom could clearly be seen and looked uncomfortably close.

"Two fathoms, but it's getting shallower," said Peter.

"What do the charts show?"

"Fifteen to twenty feet."

"We should be OK then. Keep your eye on the echo sounder."

For an hour Beth sailed lazily into the calm evening – the widening vee of her wake stretching out in the distance behind her as the old bus engine pounded away, turning the big propeller.

"Steady up, Dad, we're down to half a fathom!" shouted Peter.

"What's that in feet and inches?" asked Don.

"Not much. About three feet."

"Strewth!"

"You're OK, it's getting deeper now."

"It's a good job the sea's calm. We'd have hit the bottom before now, otherwise."

Don steered Beth a little closed to the shore, looking for a place he could anchor for the night. He saw a few houses on a beach a little way ahead.

"What's that place, Peter?"

"It's only a village. You can't stop there."

"I just want to anchor for the night. What's it called?"

"It could be Bonassa," said Peter. "But it's not very clear on the chart."

"Right, we'll get as close as we can and drop the hook. I'm gasping for a Coke; perhaps we can get some here."

Half an hour later the anchor was down and the engine silent. The only noise to be heard was the chugging of a small boat, coming towards them from the beach. There were two men in the boat.

"Where you from, man?" shouted one of the men in the dinghy.

"England," said Don. "What's this place called?"

"Bonassa. You come from England in that?" The man asked, incredulously.

"That's right."

"You're crazy, man," said the Trinidadian.

"Are you coming ashore?" asked the other man.

"We can't. We have to see the customs first, at Point Fortin."

"Don't worry about the customs, man. My brother is a customs officer; I'll fix it for you."

"I don't think I should," said Don.

"Come on, man. We've got stuff ashore that you need; fresh fish, bread, milk and Coca-Cola."

"Hey, did you say Coca-Cola?"

"That's right, man. We got Coke, 7up, beer."

"That settles it. Look after things aboard, Peter. I'm going ashore to get some Coke."

Trinidad, having been a British administered island at one time, presented no language problem and the people were extremely friendly.

Don bought his Coca-Cola and also a bucket of the most delicious prawns from the fishermen and returned to Beth. Lena took charge of the prawns and cooked them for the crew, making a delicate change from the meals they had eaten during the crossing. They could not stay at Bonossa as it was only a beach and had no facilities; they were also breaching the law, so in the morning they said farewell to the fishermen and headed for Point Fortin, just a little way up the coast.

It was only a short trip, and as soon as they were anchored in Point Fortin Don went through the correct procedure of raising the yellow quarantine flag and waiting for the authorities. It was not long before a customs officer came out to Beth, and Don noted that it was the only time so far, apart from Gibraltar, that the authorities had taken notice of the procedure.

When the man from the customs had gone, Don went ashore and presented the usual papers and passports and was given clearance.

The Caisleys found the people in Trinidad extremely friendly. Not just the fishermen of Bonassa, but everybody they met, from the local newspaper reporters to the men working in the dockyard. They were warm and genuine, and made the family welcome.

One afternoon, after showing a group of inquisitive dockyard workers around the boat, Don was asked if he had heard of 'Sparrow'.

"Sparrow?"

"Yeah, man, Sparrow. A calypso singer. He's great."

Apparently, Sparrow was a local celebrity and very much in vogue at the time.

"No, I never have," said Don.

"You got a record player, man?"

"Yes."

"Can we bring some records over?"

"Of course, we'd be delighted," said Lena. "It'll be a change to hear something different." She was thinking of all the times she had heard 'A life on the ocean wave' from Jonathan's record player.

When the workers had gone to get their records, Lena got busy in the galley preparing food. She turned the visit into something of an occasion and the impromptu soiree was a complete success. Everybody had a good time, singing and listening to the calypsos and steel bands.

During the party one man talked to Don about his relations in Grenada, after he had heard that Beth would be calling there. He told Don that his uncle, who was a solicitor, would be pleased to see them, especially as he would be bringing news from Trinidad. Don and Lena promised they would go and visit him when they got to Grenada.

During the course of the voyage, the Caisleys met many people and lots of promises were made to write when they got to Australia, or to visit or get in touch with people in various places. Most of those promises were broken, as they were made on the spur of the moment and during entertainment of one sort or another. The promise to visit the solicitor in Grenada however, was kept.

From Point Fortin, Beth sailed to Port of Spain – the capital of Trinidad. The 70 mile journey was made pleasant by fine weather and calm seas in the Gulf of Paria. After the formalities were attended to, Don and Lena visited the Flying Angel - by this time a firmly established routine at any port where the mission was represented.

As well as being busy at sea, Lena's time was also fully occupied when Beth was alongside. There was all the heavy washing that had accumulated since the last port of call - fresh water was used very sparingly at sea. Laundry generally had to be done ashore, at a

Laundromat or sometimes at the Flying Angel or wherever else offered such facilities. All the family clothes mending had to be attended to, and catering and provisioning was a major job as there was no chance to pop out to the corner store or the local supermarket in the middle of the ocean. A couple of days before sailing, the list of provisions would be drawn up. Don helped out with the quantities because he knew roughly how long Beth would be at sea.

A typical shopping list was the one in Trinidad, restocking after the Atlantic crossing:

36 tins	Ass. cans fruit
12	Luncheon meat ea. 2lb
110 lb	Potatoes
2 case	Coca Cola
4 bot.	Rum
60 lb	Carrots
1 case	Apples
5 lb	Ass. macaroni
20 tins	Whole tomatoes
10 lb	Parmesan cheese
10 tins	Table butter
12 tins	Frankfurters
5 lb	Margarine
4 gals.	Orange syrup
4 bots.	Lime cordial
20 nos.	Limes
16 ltrs	Stayfresh milk
10 pkts.	Cornflakes
4gls.	Teepol
48 pcs.	Cadbury chocolates
26 lb	Bananas
15 lb	Bacon
3 dz.	Eggs large A grade

7 lb	Chicken
6 Lvs.	Bread
1 tin	Cookies
5pkts.	Flour each 51b.
1 only	Panamanian flag
1 only	Venezuelan flag
10 pcs.	Lux toilet soap,
6 pkts.	Breeze
1 case	Carib beer

The preparation of the shopping list entailed a lot more care than just getting the quantities right. Grocery shopping was a relatively simple matter - it was the little incidental items that could cause problems. Beth was at sea for over 21 days crossing the Atlantic and the stowage space aboard Beth was limited – so the catering had to fairly accurate.

Trinidad is an island of 1980 square miles, with a colorful history. It was discovered by Christopher Columbus on his third voyage across the Atlantic, and on that voyage he had vowed to dedicate his first landfall to the Holy Trinity hence the name 'La Trinidad', which means in Spanish, The Trinity. The British took possession of the island in 1797 and administered it until 1962, when it was granted independence. Its people – less than one million, are of mixed races and form a happy united society. Don and his family saw and heard the steel bands and enjoyed the calypsos - for which Trinidad is famous, during their three day visit to the island and its happy go lucky people.

While in Port of Spain the Caisleys met some of the crew of a British ship, the 'Planesman', which was docked there, and were invited on board to a party. One character they remember very well was the chief engineer whose forte was playing the mouth organ with his nose, much to the delight and amusement of Jonathan. Don had been around ships and seafaring people for some time by then, and knew from his association with them that sailors are of a different breed to landlubbers. There is something about the life at sea that draws the crew of a ship together in a comradeship that is not found ashore. They also have an appreciation of the needs of other seafarers, so it was not surprising that Don should be asked by the crew of the freighter if there was anything he needed. After some minutes thought, he said,

"One thing I have really missed is an English sausage." This was a request that was easily accommodated, and the Caisleys left the Planesman with a sand bag full of sausages. Once again, during the party and having a good time, Don made a promise to write at every landfall they made enroute to Perth. The promise to the chief engineer was made in good faith, because he really intended to write when he made it, but with so much happening during the voyage it was broken.

Len, the bus driver, left Beth while they were in Port of Spain -he had been threatening to leave the boat at every big wave encountered in the Atlantic. Where he would have gone with his kit bag and life jacket during the crossing, no-one was sure. With Len gone, Beth was one man short for safe watch keeping and Jonathan then filled that position. In spite of his tender years, Jonathan was growing up fast, and he took the responsibility of a full crew member and stood his watches with the rest of them.

After three days in Port of Spain the Caisleys were ready to leave. Farewells were made, and Beth was cast off and headed out of the harbour. As they passed the

'Planesman', hooters and sirens were blasted off in a cacophonic goodbye, and soon Don and his crew were in the Gulf of Paria, with the last echoes of the noisy valediction still ringing in their ears.

The shallow water area between Trinidad and Venezuela leads out through a narrow channel to the Caribbean Sea, called the Dragon's Mouth. Unlike the Serpent's Mouth where Beth had entered the Gulf of Paria, this passageway to the sea had a channel deep enough for large ocean going vessels. This time they were heading for Saint Georges in Grenada, a distance of some 96 miles.

The weather changed dramatically once they were in the Caribbean and the seas became big and rough. The wind was whipping the white caps of the waves into a flying spume that stung the exposed flesh of the brave souls who ventured on deck, making the crossing the most uncomfortable passage Don had made so far, with Beth being tossed around like a cork.

After about three hours of the buffeting, Don was lying on his bunk feeling sick and wondering why he had ever embarked on such a crazy venture. Lena was in the galley, trying to prepare a meal - pots and pans were sliding around on the little stove, making it almost impossible to cook. She decided to leave the cooking until the sea had calmed down; however, Don was not worried about food.

As he lay clinging to the side of the bunk, the crash of the sea almost drowned out the monotonous pounding of the engine, and it seemed incredible to him that the sea could change so dramatically - from the calm waters of the Gulf of Paria a few hours ago, Beth rolled and pitched in the turbulent Caribbean. But through all the noise, Don thought he detected a change in the note of the engine, and he sat up, listening. There was something wrong: the engine still thumped on, but it sounded different.

He swung his legs off the bunk just as Ginger called down from the wheelhouse. Ginger had the helm, and he had noticed the engine temperature creeping up.

As soon as Don got to the engine room he could see where the trouble was - the link belt driving the pump that circulated cooling water over the engine had broken. The engine had got dangerously hot, and had to be shut down before serious damage was done.

The old trawler had been making life uncomfortable for the crew for several hours – but it was nothing compared to what she did when the engine was stopped. For such a short journey the sails had not been set, and without the engine she was being pushed and thrown around in all directions. Under power she pushed into the waves, and there was a pattern to the movement, however, until the belt was fixed, she was at the mercy of the sea.

Don forgot the nausea that had dominated his thoughts up until a few moments ago. The repair had to be made quickly, but it was not that easy: everything on the engine was hot – too hot to touch, and metal crackled as it cooled down. Under normal conditions changing the belt would have been a relatively easy job – but the hot engine was alive and fierce. Several times he was thrown balance and fell against the hot metal, burning his hands or arms.

Working with the urgency that the situation called for, the belt was eventually replaced, and after topping up the fresh water in the cooling system which had boiled dry, the engine was restarted. Back under power, Beth resumed her normal rolling and pitching. It was the end of a most unpleasant hour for everybody aboard.

At 8.00am on the following morning, Don brought Beth into Saint Georges harbour, Grenada, and tied up to a jetty. The Caisley's had traveled 4995 miles since leaving Southampton, and were thankful that that the last 90 miles were over.

Grenada is the southernmost of the Windward Islands which encloses the Caribbean Sea, and is about the same size physically as the Isle of Wight, from where the Caisley's journey began. It has a similar history to that of Trinidad, having been discovered in the fifteenth century by Christopher Columbus, and changed hands several times during the course of the wars between England and France in the eighteenth century.

For Don and his family it was another very pleasant and friendly stop over. During their stay they visited the yacht club, where a lot of interest was shown in Beth and the voyage they were making. They also paid a visit to the relations of the man in Point Fortin as they had promised, and were delightfully surprised by the reception they received.

The solicitor and his wife turned out to be an elderly couple - very sophisticated and 'English Colonial' in their relationship. They owned a small plantation where they grew cotton and various kinds of fruit. Don, Lena and the boys were taken on a conducted tour of the property, and as they were leaving, a pickup truck was loaded with paw paws, bananas, breadfruit, eggplants and mangoes for them to take back on board. They were entertained with much charm and hospitality and the visit stood out as one of the highlights of their stay in Grenada, of which they retain many pleasant memories.

Initially, Beth was tied up alongside a restaurant-cum-supermarket-cum-bar called the Nutmeg while in Saint Georges harbour, and later moved and anchored out in the lagoon. While the boat was tied up alongside, a young Grenadian came aboard looking for work - he wanted to sail with Beth. Don's usual prerequisites in such cases were that the applicant should pay enough for food and also provide some skills necessary in watch keeping and the normal ship board duties, while Don would provide the fuel, docking and mooring fees and other expenses involved with the boat. This particular young man had only $40 and no skills that Don wanted, except a desire to work.

After Don had taken him down to the foc'sle mess and interviewed him, he was not sure he wanted him aboard, as he could create problems in some of the ports Beth would be visiting because of his color.

Also, if he turned out to be unsatisfactory, Don was concerned that he may be responsible for his passage back to Grenada. The skipper discovered, after he had seen the man, that he had previously been seen by other members of the crew who had taken an immediate liking to him, and in fact had actually urged him to talk to Don. After the interview, the rest of the crew had then tried to persuade Don to take him aboard. The young man's name was Len Fleming, and once Don had got him to agree that, should he prove unsatisfactory for any reason, he would not hold him responsible for his return passage wherever Beth happened to be at the time, he was signed on as a crew member.

Len stayed with Beth for the rest of the voyage and although he did not have the necessary skills to begin with, was quick to learn and willing to perform any task that was set for him. He soon became a valuable member of the crew and was well liked and respected by everyone aboard. Don discovered later, that Len in his eagerness to go to sea had even joined a seaman's union, although he had never been on a ship before.

Shortly after Len signed on, Beth was moved out into the lagoon, and while there, Don and Len were scraping and painting the outside of the hull from a raft. A speed boat came racing past them at high speed, and very close. The wash swamped the raft and threw both of them into the water along with the brushes and paint and everything else that was on the raft; Don and Len were not hurt, just wet, but the paint and brushes etc. were lost. After listening to Don curse the idiot responsible - who did not stop or come back, Len discovered that the captain could get exceedingly angry, but it did not deter him from continuing as a crew member.

Among the many people the Caisleys met in Grenada was an Australian who had sailed the world in a yacht, and Don and he swapped yarns of their experiences. The Australian, who owned a very large .45 six shooter, told Don of the time in South Africa when he caught an intruder on his yacht, held him with the gun, and finally marched him off to the authorities with his hands in the air, whereupon he was arrested with the intruder for possessing firearms. Don remembered an incident a few nights earlier in Port of Spain, when he found someone on the upper deck and challenged him with his .22 air pistol. The man, whoever he was, did not stop to identify himself and Don fired a slug in his direction. The slug hit some metal object and the whining sound of the ricochet must have put the fear of God into the man because he was off the boat and over an eight feet high wire fence as though he had sprouted wings. During the discussion on firearms with the Australian, Don traded a bayonet he had - which fitted an older type of .303 rifle, for some ammunition to fit his current rifle. Trade in ammunition and firearms among seafaring people is common, he found out.

For part of their stay in Grenada, Don and Lena engaged a taxi driver to take them around the beaches and other interesting places. The taxi driver, named LeRoy, was a well known character and he spent a full day taking them to beaches, local beauty spots and places of interest while telling them stories about Grenada. After eight days they had seen almost all there was to see of the tiny island, and Don had done all the maintenance that was necessary.

The fuel and water tanks were filled and provisions taken aboard, then a course was plotted that would take Beth to Caracus in Venezuela.Don went to see the harbour authorities and gave them details of the next leg of his journey. The original plan had been to visit Barbados, but with the long loop southwards from Las Palmas, then the southerly approach to Trinidad, it was decided to press on towards Panama and the Pacific without making the detour to Barbados.

By this time the economics of the voyage were demanding more and more attention. Navigation was relegated to second place in Don's list of priorities, and the dwindling finances loomed as a major concern -

shortage of money was to be one of his main worries throughout the rest of the voyage.

*****

Don Salvages A Yacht In Cartagena

At 11.00am on the 22nd of August, Beth left Saint Georges Harbour as the Cunard liner, Adventurer, was arriving. No raging beauty, Beth looked incongruous as she passed by the graceful ship, rolling in the swell while the liner glided serenely to her mooring.

The passage to Caracas was uneventful except for one incident that involved their new crew member, Len Fleming. Len was at the helm during one of his watches, and Peter had told him to make a course correction from 240 degrees to 245. Shortly afterwards Beth was behaving in a very strange fashion. The steady pitching and rolling changed to one of violent rolling, and the sails, now empty of the life giving wind, flapped uselessly against the mast.

Don and Peter went to the wheelhouse to see what the cause of this peculiar behavior was. They thought they knew all of Beth's quirks and foibles by that time but the antics she was now performing were new to them. They found Len turning the helm in every direction but the correct one - one minute Beth was heading into the weather and the next she was beam on to the sea.

"What are you playing at?" said Don. Poor Len was so confused.

"I can't find 245 degrees on the compass." Peter started to laugh and took the helm from Len. He swung the wheel to correct the course and as Beth settled down, the compass slowly came through 250 degrees 245, and held steady.

"There you are Len, what's the problem?"

"Where's 245 degrees?" Len scratched his head and peered at the compass.

"Look, there it is, right between 240 and 250."

Don could now see what the problem was and shared in Peter's mirth. The compass was marked in 10 degree segments with all other points marked only with a dot. Len had been looking for the number 245, which was not there. He laughed at himself when the mistake was pointed out - he was still green, but he was learning. Don remembered how green he was when he purchased Beth. They had all come a long way since then and learnt a lot, but there was still a lot more to be learned. He playfully ruffled Len's hair to show him he was not annoyed by the incident, and left the wheelhouse to get back to the work he was doing in the engine room. It was late afternoon on the 24th when Beth arrived at La Guaira - which is the seaport for Caracus. As they approached from the Caribbean, the city of Caracus - some nine miles distant from La Guaira, was obscured by a range of mountains rising majestically to 3000 feet. It was a busy seaport, with ships of many nationalities loading and discharging their cargoes at the wharves. Don did not allow himself to be distracted by the grandeur of the landscape but concentrated on bringing Beth to a safe mooring. Once she was secured alongside, he busied himself with the formalities - by then almost second nature to him. Lena, after watching the activity of the harbour and the scenery as they approached, was tending to some culinary chores in the galley, and Jonathan and Peter were waiting for their father to return from the customs so they could go ashore.

Don came striding along the dockside, his gait had considerably more roll to it than a year ago, Lena thought as she watched him.

"Can we go ashore now Dad?" Jonathan was eager to be off the boat and walking on the more substantial terra firma.

"We can go ashore alright, but only to look. The banks are closed and I haven't got any Venezuelan money until tomorrow." He was annoyed that he had not converted some money before they left Grenada. "We can't all go. Someone has to stay and look after Beth." Peter and Jonathan had already jumped onto the dockside.

"Mum said she will wait until tomorrow and Len doesn't want to go." Peter was also glad to be standing on something that did not slide out from under his feet at the merest breeze.

The three of them set off along the dockside, past enormous warehouses with corrugated iron sides, indistinguishable from dockside buildings anywhere else in the world. Out through the main gate of the docks were a few drab houses, a cafe here and there, and the inevitable murky jumble of buildings associated with the shipping trade. Everywhere the peculiar smell of marine commerce pervaded the air until, from a small cafe, just outside the main gate, an aroma that came wafting on

129

the evening breeze had them savoring the air like the 'Bisto Kids' - it was the most delicious smell of fried chicken that had them drooling.

"You would like some chicken?" It was meant as a question, but was the truest statement possible. The voice came from behind them in Spanish, which Don understood - he was reasonably conversant with the language from his trucking days.

"We would love some, but we've got no money until tomorrow."

"That's OK, are you from an English ship?" Don explained how he and his family had just arrived in La Guaira. "That's OK; you will be here tomorrow and can pay then. You can come in now and have what you want," the man from the cafe told them. The offer was too good to refuse, so into the cafe they went and sat down to a delicious feast of fried chicken. When they left, they took some back to Lena and the others who agreed it was the best fried chicken they had ever tasted.

La Guaira, like any other seaport, is not the most romantic place with its lofty cranes, rather dilapidated corrugated iron warehouses, dirty wharves and always the conglomeration of smells peculiar to the shipping industry. It was however, the seaport serving Caracas, the capital city of Venezuela - the country which has grown fabulously wealthy over the past 50 years or so through its discovery and sale of oil, and was at that time the second largest oil producer in the world. As the Caisleys traveled along the Autopista on the bus the day after their arrival in Venezuela, they marveled at the effort and cost of that beautiful road, one of the finest motor roads in the world, as it passed through tiled and illuminated tunnels cut through mountains and across enormous ravines spanned by concrete bridges.

From sea level the road climbed 3000 feet to the city of Caracas, behind which another range of mountains formed a scenic backdrop. In the capital they saw where a lot of the oil money had been spent - vast areas of skyscrapers in the downtown section of Caracas dominated the skyline. They expected to see some of the old buildings in a city with a history going back to 1767, but saw very few. In the Plaza Bolivar - which is beautifully paved with mosaics, a few of the old buildings were still standing, however, most of the workers shacks had been cleared to make way for huge blocks of flats and apartments. Where they did see shacks - mainly on the outskirts of the city and the mountain sides, the contrast was stark poverty in the midst of such affluence.

To visit such places was an education, and Jonathan - who would normally have been attending school had they remained in England, was gaining a far richer and broader experience of the world and its people than most other boys of his age. He was also doing his normal lessons as they traveled with Beth.

As they were strolling around Caracas taking in the sights, Lena stepped on a banana skin that had been carelessly thrown on the sidewalk, and she went down in a most unladylike manner that had Don and the boys laughing. Lena however, was not amused, she had hurt her toe rather badly - it turned out later that she had broken it. Don helped her to her feet and took her into what looked like a café, however, they had an even bigger laugh when they had got Lena sitting down; the 'cafe', they discovered, did not serve tea and cakes in the normal course of business - it was a brothel! Lena was in pain and in no mood to be dragged around while a more salubrious venue was found - her agony demanded immediate attention. The girls who staffed the establishment were hospitable and kind, even though it was obvious that they would not do any business with these tourists. Some ice was found and a compress made for Lena's foot. It eased the pain and after thanking the girls, Don helped his wife out of the chair and left with the boys – the broken toe gave Lena a lot of pain and she was hobbling around for weeks afterward.

Back aboard Beth, Don was notified by the harbour authorities that the President's yacht was due to arrive soon and would require the berth that Beth occupied. The old trawler was directed to a mooring on the other side of the harbour, and Don cast off as soon as everybody was on board and moved to the berth he was given, alongside an Indian boat. When he got there, Don found the skipper of the Indian boat had also been moved and was manoeuvring his boat to tie up against the jetty. Don politely backed off until the other boat had completed berthing, then came alongside and tied up. The two captains were soon discussing the move the move they had just made and the impending arrival of the Venezuelan President and the Indian skipper invited Don and Lena to dinner that evening. The meal was a fairly lavish affair - the sumptuous trappings of the Indian boat took Don and Lena by surprise, after the matter-of-fact and utilitarian fittings of Beth. After the meal they were taken on a conducted tour of the boat, Lena noticing the staterooms and galley while Don's interest centered mainly on the engine room.

With Lena's native Italian language and Don's knowledge of French, communication was not a big problem in foreign ports. They got to know many of the Venezuelan people and managed to converse intelligently with them – especially one young man named Jesus, a crewman from the President's yacht. They spent a long time in interesting discussion and learned a lot about Venezuela. The customs officials were regular visitors, not on official business, but just friendly visits showing interest in 'those crazy English people' and what they were doing. Don would have liked to stay longer as the family had built up a rapport with the local people, but money was becoming a problem - the longer they stayed ashore, the more it cost. Don was already way over the costs he had budgeted for so it was imperative to move on, and dwindling finances would now dictate the length of stay in the places visited throughout the rest of the voyage. The next port of call would be Cartagena in Colombia, before the Panama Canal and the Pacific Ocean.

Beth slipped out of La Guaira harbour early on the morning of the 30th of August and headed westward. Don intended to follow the coast, keeping as close inshore as was safely possible. Coastal navigation was easy in daylight when the coast and the way ahead could clearly be seen, but at night and without radar, it was a different proposition. Beth had all the equipment essential for safe navigation but she was not fitted with radar, and as she was sailing close to the coast, Don decided he would travel only by day. At 7.30pm on the first day out of La Guiara, he dropped anchor. Early the next morning the anchor was raised and Beth continued her journey until the evening when she was anchored offshore again.

On the 1st of September, Aruba Island was sighted off the starboard beam and by the 2nd they were in Colombian waters. On the evening of the 3rd at 9pm Beth was anchored off Point Caruso, and the log showed that 615 miles had been covered since leaving La Guiara. By the late evening of the 4th they were off Cartegena, but there was not a direct route from the sea into that harbour. Cartegena is situated at the northern end of the Bay of Cartagena and can only be reached through a narrow channel having its entrance at Boca Chica, some 30 miles to the south.

Early on the morning of the 5th the anchor was raised and Beth proceeded down the coast to the entrance of the water-way to Cartagena. Don had to refer most carefully to his pilot book - the entrance was narrow with treacherous mud banks on either side. The waterway itself was deceptive, with patches of shallow and deep water. At one point Don ran Beth aground, but as her speed was greatly reduced, by immediately running the engine astern, it was possible to slide off the mud. No damage was done and no embarrassment caused by having to wait, helpless, until the tide changed or some other vessel came to their assistance.

The entrance and the channel to Cartegena were once heavily fortified against such adventurers as John Hawkins and his pupil, Francis Drake. Some of those old fortresses still remain and stand as stark reminders of the past. As he piloted Beth up the channel, Don inwardly applauded the actions of those audacious men who sailing into uncharted seas with only surprise and courage on their side, fought and conquered, bringing back the spoils to their queen.

The historic city of Cartagena was founded in 1533 and was known as Cartagena de Indies, in order to differentiate it from the Spanish city of the same name. The area was rich in gold and silver, and from its founding, the Spanish sent great fleets of galleons to collect that wealth and transport it back to Spain. Activity which did not go unnoticed - it attracted the attention of every pirate and buccaneer on the Spanish Main. During the 17th century, a wall - which still stands today, was built around the city to protect it from such marauders. Once the centre for the Inquisition and a major market for Negro slaves, Cartagena is now Colombia's major port for the export of liquid gold – oil.

After a relatively slow passage through the channel, Beth entered Cartagena harbour and was tied up close to a motor yacht named Gypsy. As soon as they were berthed and the formalities had been attended to, the Caisleys went ashore to stretch their legs and have a look around. The boat, Gypsy, they were moored near was owned by an American, Lloyd and his wife Georgina. After introductions and general pleasantries Don discovered they had been in Cartagena for three months, could speak the language and were fairly knowledgeable about the area. It was not long before Don and Lloyd got to discussing boats and sailing and swapping salty yarns. Lloyd told Don that during the time he had been in Cartegena, his boat had become encrusted with barnacles and marine growth below the waterline, to the point where it was a major job to clear it. Don offered to have a look at it, always looking for a way to earn a little money to help out with the dwindling finances. The offer was accepted and Don put on his diving gear and went down to inspect the hull of the yacht. What he found surprised him - the hull was one thick mass of barnacles and the propeller was covered to a depth of four to five inches. It would take days to clear it, he reported back to Lloyd. Time was not a major consideration for either man, and so Don took on the job. After three days of chipping and scraping under water, he had the hull and propeller clear. Don and Lloyd became good friends and Don did several jobs on Gypsy during their stay in Cartagena.

The Caisleys met many friendly people in Cartagena and during conversation with some of them one day, the subject of a yacht that had sunk at her mooring in the yacht pens came up. Don was interested, and Lloyd took him over to have a look at it. The yacht was sitting on the bottom and at low water the top of the cockpit was almost surfaced.

Lloyd told Don that several estimates of the cost to raise the yacht had been tendered – however, they were all in the four figure bracket.

"It doesn't look too difficult to me," said Don, whose brain was working overtime at ways he could raise it with his own equipment. On the way back to Beth with Lloyd, Don had the solution.

"Lloyd, I could raise that yacht with the gear I've got on Beth." Lloyd was skeptical at first, but he had seen Don go to work on his boat, and finish the jobs he set out to do.

"Do you honestly think that you could raise her without specialized equipment?"

"Yes, I'm sure I could." Don outlined his thoughts on the salvage to Lloyd.

"Let's go and talk to the harbormaster. He's pretty keen to clear that pen and there could be a few dollars in it for you." Lloyd was aware of Don's financial deficiency. They both went over to the harbormaster's office and Don put his proposal.

"No, I don't think you could do it. You have to have the proper equipment, because it's a very specialized job." Lloyd translated for Don and the harbormaster. Don was adamant that the job was not beyond his capability and he finally convinced the harbormaster to let him try.

Soon the news got around the harbour that he was going to try and raise the yacht, and the following morning there was a large group of spectators as Don and Peter set to work.

First they built up the cockpit with a box arrangement so that it was clear of the water. Then all the entries where water could get in had to be sealed off. Don put on his diving gear and went down into the sunken yacht and closed all the scuppers and portholes. Then all the vents and deck holes, such as the anchor chain hole had to be sealed. They worked quickly and efficiently together and when they were satisfied that the yacht was sealed, the intake hose was run from Beth's fire pump and the pump started. They were making good progress, with the pump gaining on the water that was slopping through the extended combing.

Unfortunately Don had not reckoned on the time of the tides changing, and it was the tide that beat them on that first attempt. Before the yacht had time to reach a state of buoyancy the rising tide flooded over the top of the combing they had made around the cockpit. As the tide beat them there was a lot of laughter from the spectators and Lloyd said to Don

"Do you still think you can do it?"

Don was more determined than ever that not only could he do it, but he would have the yacht floating the next day.

"The tide starts out at 4.00am tomorrow morning and by 6.00am the box around the cockpit will be clear and Peter and I will be ready. We'll have her afloat by the time the tide turns again."

Lloyd wished he could be as certain that the job would be done, but he kept his thoughts to himself.

The next morning, Don and Peter had Beth in position by the sunken yacht, and by the time the hoses had been rigged, the box combing around the cockpit of the yacht was above the surface. The fire pump was started and began sucking water out of the boat. Within a couple of hours it was obvious that the pump was gaining on the water - another two hours and the yacht stirred from the bottom. The tide was no problem now; the yacht was afloat and would rise with the tide. They kept the pump running until the hose was sucking air in the bilges and the yacht was completely clear of water.

"I must confess Don, I didn't think you could do it. Let's go and see the harbormaster." Lloyd said.

The laughter and shouting from the spectators was no longer derisory, as it had been the previous day.

"If you put your mind to it, you can do anything. What do you say Peter?" Don put his arm across Peter's shoulder and they walked to the harbormaster's office with Lloyd.

The harbormaster was pleased. He should have been - he had been quoted thousands of dollars to raise the yacht.

"Very, very good. I wouldn't have thought it possible with your equipment," he said. "I'll stop by your boat this evening and reckon up with you." Lloyd translated.

Don was pleased: he had not given a price for the job, but he knew what it was worth and expected at least a few hundred dollars which would have helped the Caisley finances a great deal. That evening the harbormaster called at Beth with the payment for Don and Peter's work. It was not a few hundred dollars, and it was not even cash - the recompense for the salvage of the yacht was two bottles of rum!

Don, normally a voluble person, was so flabbergasted as to be temporarily stuck for words; however, finally he managed to splutter:

"I don't believe this, we salvage a £20,000 yacht and you pay two bottles of rum!" That was it, the harbormaster shrugged his shoulders and left. He would not even waive the mooring fees that Beth was running up.

"We might as well drink the rum, Peter, grab some glasses," said Don.

Drink the rum they did, with Lloyd and a few other friends and the more they drank, the more inebriated they became and the more abuse they heaped on the harbormaster until finally the rum was all gone. By next morning most of their disappointment and resentment had abated and just a hangover remained.

The hangover had gone by lunchtime and Lloyd suggested they all go out for the evening.

"How about the cinema?" said Lena.

"Now there's a good idea, and afterwards we can go for a meal, my treat." Lloyd still felt bad about the previous afternoon: he felt partly responsible as it was he had put the suggestion to the harbormaster.

The old absorption refrigerator that Don had installed during the refit was not coping! In fact, it had never been satisfactory because it would work only in harbour or dead calm conditions – something Beth rarely encountered. Even in Southampton - where the average temperatures are generally higher than the rest of England, the old fridge was barely adequate.

In Cartagena – although still in the Northern Hemisphere, the average high temperature ranged from 30°C to 24°C year round. To exacerbate the problem, August is in the rainy season with humidity around 70%, going as high as 90%, so a more efficient refrigerator was sorely needed. The problem was to find one that worked on the compression principal and ran from 12 volts DC, and when Don was told of a way to get standard AC model running from 12volts DC, he jumped at it. The mechanic who had mentioned it said they should buy an old domestic refrigerator and he would convert it.

After Don had purchased an old compression refrigerator, the mechanic spent two days, unsuccessfully, trying to make the conversion. It was obvious to Don that the man didn't know what he was doing and the conversion was not going to be a success. Eventually the mechanic left Beth with the job incomplete. The man was not paid for his work because he had not finished what he had contracted to do. The old refrigerator would not work and could only be used as a storage cupboard.

Little more was thought about the matter until the day Beth was leaving Cartegena when two policemen arrived at the mooring to arrest Don for not paying the mechanic. Fortunately Lloyd was onboard Beth at the time and went to the court house with him and explained to the magistrate, in his own language, what had happened regarding the conversion of the refrigerator. Up to then, the court had heard only the mechanic's side of the story. As the full facts became known, the tables were turned and it was the mechanic's turn to be arrested for fraud! The magistrate made him apologize publicly for trying to defraud the Caisleys, who didn't want to press charges. They had made a lot of friends and did not want to leave with any hard feelings about the refrigerator or the floating of the yacht.

While Don and the boys were working on Beth or some other boat, Lena and Georgina used to go shopping. Mostly they went to the American services base, but sometimes they would go to the local markets which Lena found to be quite an education. On one occasion while shopping for fresh vegetables, dodging the flies and the countless small children racing around, she noticed two scruffy little urchin boys harassing a man - one boy was in front of him while the other boy was behind. The boy behind had whipped out a razor blade and slit the man's trouser pocket while his attention was on the boy in front, and stolen his wallet. Both boys then ran off into the market throng and disappeared. It had all happened so fast that Lena had no time to call out and warn the man. Those little rogues could not have been more than ten or eleven years old, yet they were expert thieves.

Eduardo, the son of the British Consul in Cartagena was another of the friends the Caisley family made while in Colombia, and Eduardo would have more reason to remember Don than most. He had an old boat and was trying to get it seaworthy. The engine was absolutely useless, and he had obtained another engine which he was trying to overhaul before fitting it in the boat. The replacement engine had seized solid and he had asked Don if he could help.

Don was always ready to oblige and he soon had the engine apart, except for the pistons which had really welded themselves in the bores - the only way to shift them was to knock them out with a large hammer and a piece of wood. Eduardo held the block of the engine and a piece of wood on the bottom of a piston, while Don swung a 14 pound hammer at the wood. The work was proceeding well until, for some inexplicable reason, Eduardo moved his head right in the path of the falling hammer and caught the full force of it on his nose! Poor Edward, he lay there fully conscious, blubbering through his smashed lips and nose - his features were a mess, scaring Don out of his wits as his face was a bloody pulp. Don and Peter picked him up and rushed with him on board Beth, laying him on the wardroom table.

Lying alongside Beth was a boat called Spray belonging to a Dr. Doug Campbell and Peter raced across and asked the doctor if he would come and help Eduardo. By the time Doug Campbell arrived, Eduardo - still laying on the wardroom table, had collected quite a sizeable audience what with Lloyd, the Caisleys and other crew members all trying to give moral support but none daring to touch in case they made things worse.

They quickly cleared a space for the doctor who proceeded with the business of trying to reconstruct Edward's face from the mess of flesh and bone the hammer had left. With no local anaesthetic, Dr Campbell cleaned him up so he could see what was left for him to work with, then pulled what remained of his nose out of the middle of the pulpy mess. With expert manipulation of the remains of the nose and tacking in a few deft stitches to hold it all together, the doctor worked to reconstruct the patient's face. The rest of the operation didn't take long, and after an anti-tetanus injection, Eduardo was helped off the table and taken home.

With such an injury, Don didn't think he would see him again - they were intending to leave Cartagena in a week's time. Imagine everybody's surprise a few days later, when Eduardo showed up aboard Beth! Apart from two black eyes and the stitches sprouting out of his face and nose like thick black bristles, he looked almost recovered.

Before leaving Cartagena, Don filled his fuel and water tanks to capacity and he also purchased a large stock of Coca-Cola - both oil and 'Coke' were extremely cheap by comparison with other places they had stayed. He also took on three passengers who could stand watches with the rest of the crew - they were two English boys, out for some adventure and seeing the world, and a Chilean who had escaped from his own country. All three wanted to go to America and told Don they had the necessary papers. Naturally, Don checked with the U.S. Consul in Cartagena that it was in order to take such passengers to America, and they were satisfied as long as the boys had sufficient money for their fares home should they not be allowed into the USA.

*****

Beth Rolls Over In Balboa

At 3.00pm on the 19th of September, Beth slipped her mooring and made her way down the channel, through the marker buoys, to Boca Chica. By early evening, they were in the Caribbean en-route for the Panama Canal, course 255 degrees. The following day, with 130 miles on the log since leaving Colombia, the sea was mirror calm and the sun shone out of a flawless blue sky. Don wished it could always be that way - remembering the journey to Grenada. He stopped the engine and gave the boys a chance for a little relaxation - a swim around the boat. They had been warned about sharks in the area so Don took the precaution of sitting on the wheelhouse roof with his .303 rifle while the boys were in the water. After about half an hour they climbed back aboard and Beth continued on her way.

It was a very pleasant part of the voyage, they were in coastal waters, the sea was dead calm and the weather fine and sunny. The off watch members of the crew were relaxed and looking forward to the exciting passage through the Panama canal – one of the engineering wonders of the world.

"Ginger, they'll not let you through the Panama Canal with hair like that," somebody said in the foc'sle.

"What can I do about it, there isn't a barber onboard!" Ginger retorted. He didn't want to lose his fair locks after all the time it had taken him to grow them so long.

"I'll cut your hair for you," offered Lena. After all, she had cut hair for Don and the boys enough times. After some thought, Ginger reluctantly agreed and he sat down with a cloth around his neck while Lena started to snip away at his golden curls. Snip, snip, snip, Ginger sat patiently while Lena worked around him. It did not seem to be going right - the trouble was, with the motion of the boat she was finding it difficult to cut even. As fast as she balanced one side the other looked lopsided. By the time she had finished there was enough hair on the deck to stuff a cushion, and Ginger had had a crew cut!

Early on the morning of the 21st they were passing Francis Drake's last resting place - Nombre de Dios, and at 11.30.am Beth entered Colon harbour and into the Panama Canal traffic system. They were met by a U.S. coastguard boat as the yellow quarantine flag was being raised. The coastguard directed Beth to a buoy, where they moored while Don went through the customs formalities.

The Panama Canal authorities have extremely stringent procedures for vessels in Canal transit, and as all boats and ships using the Canal must have a pilot, and the transit time is usually between seven and eight hours for the 40 mile journey, a holding area is provided. On the Caribbean side of the Canal, it is Cristobal on Limon Bay; and it was there that Don berthed Beth on the 22nd, at a yacht club mooring.

Once in Cristobal, Don had to go to the Panama Canal authorities and present them with Beth's vital statistics and certification. When that was done, it was just a matter of waiting in line until it was Beth's turn to take on the pilot and proceed through the Canal. Three days after Beth moored in Cristobal at 7.30am on the 25th, the American pilot boarded. The anchor was raised and Beth proceeded into the Canal proper.

The first locks encountered were at Gatun - three locks, one after the other, which raise the ship up to the level of the Gatun Lake, some 85 feet. Don and the boys gazed at the enormous gates as they approached.

"What would happen if a big ship came into the lock too fast and rammed the gates?" Peter asked the pilot.

"If a ship was to do what you suggested, a major disaster would result, with billions of tons of water being released to the lower levels. It couldn't happen though, because there are some big chains coupled to hydraulic springs that automatically protect the gates. They're raised as a ship approaches the gates, and then lowered before the ship moves through. The chains will stop a 10,000 ton ship moving at four knots, in 70 feet," the pilot told them.

The pilot was a mine of information about the Canal – that was when he wasn't biting his nails and worrying. He fussed around the wheelhouse, telling Don to reduce speed even further. Beth was only just moving at the time - any slower and she would lose steerage way.

"Stop engine!" The pilot shouted to Don, who thought he noticed a slight edge to his voice. The two big gates slowly swung open and Beth moved into the first Gatun lock. When they were in the lock, the gates closed behind them and the water level was raised to match the level on the other side of the far gates. All the time the pilot displayed an air of nervousness, worrying over nothing, it seemed to Don.

The Panama Canal was opened for traffic on August 15th 1914, and since then millions of tons of shipping has passed through, cutting the long journey between the Atlantic and the Pacific oceans. The locks can accommodate ships up to 1000ft long, and are 110ft wide. The four gates on the locks are each 65ft wide and 7ft thick, varying in height from 42 to 82ft, and weighing between 400 and 700 tons. They are moved by a 25HP motor through delicate gearing. Don and the boys were impressed by all the information, gradually extracted from the pilot in between his nail biting and fretting. What he did not tell them was that the Panama Canal is situated in one of the highest rainfall areas in the world - 400 inches a year is not uncommon, but they suspected as much because the rain was torrential. The warm tropical rain was coming down in 'stair rods', making deck heads and bulkheads, in fact, everything sticky and most uncomfortable in the heavy clammy atmosphere.

Once through the Gatun locks the pilot began to get even more agitated as they moved slowly into the Gatun Lake, calling all the time to his colleagues on a hand held radio. The visibility was poor and the deluge had increased. Water was running everywhere, even between decks did not escape the wet. In the lake - which appeared to Don to be more like a swamp, the channels were marked with buoys every half mile or so, and with the rain coming down so heavily, visibility was getting even worse. The pilot directed Don to a buoy, where Beth would wait until the next buoy was sighted through the rain. The log recorded '1330hrs circling a buoy waiting for the rain to ease'.

By 2.30pm Beth was out of the lake and entering Calebra Cut - now called Gaillard Cut, a colossal man-made excavation. From Calebra Cut, past Darien and Gamboa to the Pedro Miguel locks, then through the Miraflores locks, the torrential rain still making the passage anything but comfortable. Despite the discomfort, the crew still had to be fed and Lena had been busy in her small galley preparing a mouth watering roast lunch - which the pilot was to share, much to his surprise and delight.

By the evening Don had dropped the pilot and anchored four miles out of Balboa - which is the Pacific terminus for the Panama Canal. He needed a few days to make repairs and clean up Beth before continuing the voyage. The monsoon rains encountered in the canal had caused problems with the main electrical regulator, and apart from the mess on the upper deck, the interior needed drying out and cleaning. Another problem which had shown up in the canal was the variable pitch propeller, which had been sluggish and slow to respond. Even when it did respond, it didn't always do so in quite the manner it was expected to.

By this time the Caisley funds were getting embarrassingly low - they had spent far more than had been budgeted for and had covered barely a third of the journey. Don went ashore to a bank in Balboa and sent a telex to the Commonwealth Bank in Perth, to where he had transferred money prior to leaving England. He desperately needed money before leaving the canal and the telex was a request for funds to be transferred to Balboa.

While waiting for an answer from the bank, Don set to work with the rest of the crew to clean Beth inside and out, and make the necessary repairs. The electrical trouble caused by the monsoon rain had to be repaired on board as the regulator that Don required was not available in Balboa. He stripped down the faulty one and repaired it, and when it was reinstalled, sealed it with Plasticine.

The variable pitch propeller was a much bigger problem - it entailed diving below Beth and making an inspection under water. Don put on his diving gear and went over the side to take a look. What he found dismayed even him. The propeller was held to the shaft by a large boss, or hub, through which four large bolts secured it. One of the bolts was missing, and Don assumed it had dropped off while Beth was being manouevered in the Panama Canal. He removed one of the remaining bolts, leaving one each side of the hub, and returned to the surface. The bolt was 10 inches long with a diameter of 1½ inches, and had a very fine thread - it was not a standard size and meant a replacement would have to be specially made; probably at great expense. Don tried all the marine engineering workshops in Balboa and was not particularly surprised when he could not obtain a replacement. Next he went along to the yacht club, where he had already made a few friends during the short time Beth had been in Balboa. One man, an American named Dan, later nicknamed 'Desperate Dan' by the Caisleys, took a look at the bolt and said he could get one made with no trouble at all. He would have to take the bolt as a pattern.

Don was reluctant to part with the bolt - how was he to be sure he would ever see Dan or the bolt again? But he was in big trouble without a replacement, and so he gave the bolt to Dan and arranged to see him the following day for a progress report.

At lunchtime the next day, he went along to the yacht club to see Dan, optimistically hoping for the best but with a nagging worry at the back of his mind that the news would be bad. How surprised he was when Dan was not only waiting for him, but had a replacement bolt. He gave it to Don - it was a beautiful job, skillfully made in stainless steel and perfectly matched the original in every respect except the material from which it was turned.

"I'm sorry I couldn't get an exact match on the material, but it should be as strong as the others," Dan apologized. Don was ecstatic, and then the cost crossed his mind.

"It's perfect. I don't know how to thank you. Er...., how much do I owe you?" Don was holding the bolts in one hand while the fingers of the other hand were crossed as he asked the question.

"Ten dollars to you," said Dan. Not in all Don's wildest dreams would he have thought the vital bolt would have cost so little. He gladly paid there and then and invited Dan to sample the Caisley hospitality and the best meal Lena could prepare.

Don hurried back to Beth and soon had his diving gear on and was working on the propeller. The new bolt fitted perfectly and within an hour all four bolts were in and secured. He was sure the propeller bolt had caused the problems in the Canal; however, it had been fixed, and he erased that particular worry from his mind.

The financial worry remained, because there was no answer to his telex to the Commonwealth Bank in Australia. The mooring in Balboa was expensive and the longer he remained there, the more it would cost. He sent another telex, urgently requesting an answer to the first.

While he had been under Beth replacing the propeller bolts, he had noticed that the bottom of the boat was badly fouled with marine growth. It would slow Beth's progress through the water, so he decided to scrape it clean while he was waiting for his money to be transferred from Australia.

"Why don't you take it over to the other side of the Canal and lay it against the wreck? You can scrape her clean and anti-foul at the same time," somebody suggested at the yacht club, when Don mentioned what he was going to do. Don was interested because to scrape under Beth would have taken him a week.

"Where is the wreck?" he asked. He was told that on the other side of the canal was an old sunken barge that had been used in the construction of the Panama Canal. At low water the barge was completely high and dry, but could not be seen when the tide was full. Many of the yacht club members used it to lay their boats against, so they could work on them below the waterline. Don would have to get one of the locals to take him to the wreck; local knowledge was needed to be able to locate it at high water.

Don found a local guide who agreed to take him over, and told him to be ready the following afternoon at 4.00pm. The time was important because the tides moved very quickly around the wreck, and Beth had to be in position while there was still enough water to manoeuvre.

It was 4.30pm the next day when the pilot eventually showed up, and that meant getting over to the wreck as quickly as possible, half an hour had already been wasted. With the pilot on board Don raced - if one could call Beth's full nine knots racing, over to the spot where he had been directed. When they arrived, the tide was already moving and parts of the barge could be seen above the surface of the water. Beth had a weight distribution such that she tended to lean to starboard and Don wanted to lean that side against the barge. The side nearest to the barge as Beth approached it was the port side, but before Don could turn her into position she was aground. The speed of the tide was such that water was rushing between Beth and the wreck. In Don's later words, "It was just as though somebody had pulled the plug out". He could not lean Beth on the barge - she was aground and already leaning to starboard away from it. Everybody on board turned to, throwing ropes across from Beth to the barge and tying them in an effort to stop her from rolling over. The ropes began to break as Beth rolled further to starboard. There was only one chance now - cut the ropes and let her roll with the outgoing tide then pray that when the tide came in again, she would roll upright before filling with water.

Within an hour of arriving at the wreck, Beth was high and dry and over at an angle of more than 45 degrees. Fuel slopped out of the tanks, the batteries were spilling acid and everything creaked and groaned alarmingly. Lena, who had been cooking a pan of chips when they arrived at the wreck, had just time to grab the pan of hot fat and chips before they slid off the galley stove. Peter had barely enough time to get the pilot to the dinghy and back to the Balboa yacht club, and had an even more difficult task returning to Beth - he had to drag the dinghy over the expanse of mud and sand between Beth and navigable water. When he finally got back he stepped straight on to Beth, her gunwales were level with the sand.

The immediate terror of the incident had passed and it was then dark. There was nothing else anybody could do except hope and pray. Lena couldn't cook at such an angle, so it was boiled rice and bread and butter for supper. Sleeping was going to be difficult while they waited for the tide to turn - not that they felt too much like sleeping after such a frightening event. With the decks at an angle of over 45 degrees, the best they could manage was to get wedged in a corner somehow, between the deck and the bulkhead. But sleep would not come for any of them. The horror of the previous few hours was too fresh in their minds, and the worry of what might happen when the tide came in kept their senses alert and sleep from their eyes.

Lena and Jonathan wedged themselves between the sink and the bulkhead in the galley. Peter and Don scrambled around the engine room, securing the fuel tanks and cleaning up the acid spilt from the batteries. When they finally had everything secure, they found a spot where they could rest and discuss the event.

What had happened? To Don, it was painfully obvious that their guide had not realised the amount of water that Beth drew when he directed her alongside. It was basically Don's fault for not impressing on him the 11 feet of water needed. The damage was done!

All night they listened to the complaints of Beth as she lay stranded, creaking and groaning. What damage had been, and was being done, to the boat as she lay in that very unseamanlike fashion would be discovered only when the tide came back in and Beth was refloated.

It was a long and fearful night for the crew, and with the tide returning, even more worry - there was a real danger that Beth could be lost. Don had calculated that the water could slop over the gunwales and up to five feet up the deck before it reached the hatches. He hoped and prayed that Beth would right herself before then. If the incoming tide reached the hatches, Beth would fill within minutes, ending the voyage and leaving them all stranded in a strange country. With the loss of Beth their future looked bleak - all the Caisley finances were tied up in her! Don put the thoughts from his head as they were too frightening to contemplate.

Everybody was on the upper deck by 2.00am, feet wedged against some vertical protrusion and trying to stand on the wildly sloping deck, waiting for the tide and what it would bring. With the first ripple of water across the sand - indicating the returning tide, Don checked the ropes he had tied to the wreck. He hoped, by pulling towards the wreck, to assist Beth to right herself more quickly. As fast as the tide went out, so it came in. With bated breath, the Caisleys watched the water as it started to slop over the gunwales.

They hauled on the ropes, but Beth didn't move. Higher and higher rose the water and lower and lower sunk their hopes. Just another foot and the water would start flooding down the hatches. Then there was a creaking and a slight movement. Everybody redoubled their efforts on the ropes - they were going to make it!

Beth slowly moved. Her creaking got louder as the weight was lifted from the tortured timbers and the water began to recede from the hatches as slowly she righted herself.

The relief of everyone on board was apparent by their actions. Len Fleming prayed to thank God for his mercy. Jonathan cried with joy, and Lena raced to the galley to finish cooking the meal that was so frightfully interrupted the evening before. Peter and Don exhaled loudly and shook hands, laughing. When Beth was fully afloat, Don started the engine and backed her out from the wreck. Then he turned her and reversed back to the original position; but this time with the starboard side against the wreck. He had got this far and intended to do the job he had come to do in the first place. Back in position, they waited for the tide to turn. With Beth secured with a line fore and aft that was adjustable as the tide raised her above the wreck everybody turned to cleaning up the mess caused by last nights catastrophe. Don estimated they had lost around 200 gallons of fuel, but soon everything was shipshape and all the materials for scraping and antifouling lay out on the upper deck. They would have to work hard if the job was to be completed in the time it took for the tide to change.

The tide ebbed, and just as quickly as on the previous evening, the water started to rush between Beth and the wreck. There was a gentle bump as her keel made contact with the bottom and everybody held their breath - last nights terror was too real for them not to show some consternation. This time Beth was correctly positioned and as she settled on the sand, listed to starboard and leaned against the wreck. The list was no more than a few degrees, certainly not enough to cause concern or stop Lena from preparing meals, and as soon as the water had receded, work commenced. Scrape and paint, move along, scrape and paint, everybody was over the side and working. When the tide had completely left them Don inspected the hull for signs of damage, which must surely have occurred last night. He found no visible signs of damage and the scraping and painting of antifouling continued until the first ripples of water around Beth's keel told them it was time to climb back aboard. The job had not been finished, but one more tide should see it through. As the tide rose, so the securing ropes were lengthened until Beth floated above the wreck.

It was two tides later that they sailed from the wreck and to a mooring on a buoy under the canal bridge at Balboa.

"How did your careening go? I heard you had a bit of trouble out there," Dan asked when Don walked into the club.

"I don't know about careening, the bloody boat fell over!" Don told the story to his friends in the yacht club. "I reckon we've done more damage to Beth by rolling her like that than we did all the way across the Atlantic. The automatic bilge pump is going continuously, so I'm sure there must be one hell of a leak. You should have heard her creaking and groaning as she settled on her side. I was bloody terrified, I can tell you."

From the club, Don went to the bank to see if the money had arrived from Australia. It had not! In fact there had been no answer to his last two telexes. The situation regarding finance was by then reaching crisis proportions. The mooring he was on was expensive, and without funds he was worried that Beth may be impounded. He sent a third telex to the Commonwealth

Bank, stressing the urgency of his predicament. The local bank manager told him to come back again after three or four days. Meanwhile he had to repair the leaks in Beth's hull.

With Peter and Len, Don located the biggest leak. It was in the engine room, almost at the stern. It would have to be caulked from outside the hull, not a job that Don relished as he had been warned to stay out of the water in the area of the canal entrance because of sharks. Sharks or not, the leak had to be stopped - there was no question of a Pacific crossing until Beth was seaworthy. He rigged up his surface demand diving gear and prepared to go down and caulk the leak. Armed with a hammer tied to his wrist, a bunch of hemp and some red lead putty, he went over the side. He had already made some calculations of the area of the leak by measurement from inside the boat and knew approximately where the problem was.

It was difficult work - the compressor on board supplying air to his demand valve mouthpiece through a 30ft hose was blowing bits of soot and other rubbish into his mouth. It didn't take long to locate the problem area and he could then see where the planks had sprung - why could he not have spotted it when Beth was lying against the wreck? When the hemp had been hammered into the seams, he packed the red lead putty along the join, then looked all along the seams to satisfy himself that there were no other obvious places where the planks had sprung, before coming up. As he climbed back aboard, Peter and Len helped him off with his gear and reported that the leak had been stopped. For the next couple of days a careful watch was kept on the bilges, but the level was satisfactory and Don was certain that he had cured the leak.

During their enforced stay in Balboa, two of the three non-family crew had decided to leave Beth. Don was not particularly bothered - he had Len Fleming, who by this time was becoming more and more useful around the boat, as well as being a good friend. He knew also, that he could get a crew fairly easily. He posted a 'crew wanted' sign in the Balboa yacht club and soon had a number of applicants to interview.

One of the people Don had met at the club was an American army colonel, who was in charge of the local U.S. forces hospital in Balboa. He asked Don if he would take his son, Lance, as a crew member, and a canal pilot mentioned that he had a young man staying with him who was cycling around the world and would like to crew with Beth. His name was Tom and he was accepted. Another applicant, Oliver - an American, told Don he had a degree and could navigate. Finally, Don accepted a Canadian girl who had applied, because he considered it would give Lena a break – she had been providing meals for everybody since leaving England, as well as keeping her normal sea watches. With these four new crew members, Beth would have the biggest crew so far.

On the 18th of October, Don went to the bank and to his relief, the telex had been answered and the money transferred. Preparations were then made to continue the voyage. The fuel tanks were topped up; Beth had lost more than the 200 gallons that Don had estimated when she rolled over. The water tanks were filled and provisions purchased for the long Pacific crossing.

On the evening of the 19th, the day before Beth sailed, the parents of Lance were invited on board for dinner. Don went ashore in the dinghy and collected them from the jetty in Balboa. They wanted to be sure that their son would be safe and comfortable and were keen to have a good look around Beth. Don and Lena entertained them, and after a few drinks and a tour over the boat, it was time to go. Don got the dinghy ready to take them back ashore while Lance said his farewells and they exchanged presents. With his parents in the dinghy, Lance waved goodbye as Don started the outboard motor and headed for the yacht club jetty - the journey would only take ten minutes.

Halfway between Beth and the club, Don observed a large wave coming straight for the dinghy. He didn't see the ship that had caused the bow wave, but it was real enough. He turned the little boat to meet the roller bow on, but the wave was traveling fast and hit the craft before it had time to turn. Seconds later, the boat was swamped and its three occupants were in the water!

There were two lifejackets in the dinghy, and one was hastily put on the colonel's wife. The other life jacket floated away and was never recovered. Don grabbed the painter of the boat and hung on while the colonel switched on a flashlight and waved it to attract attention. Meanwhile the three of them held hands so as not to drift apart.

Don could see a freighter moored about 200yds away, and they started swimming slowly towards it, dragging the upturned boat with them. Then they heard a motor boat approaching. The colonel waved the flashlight and they all shouted to attract the attention of what turned out to be a fishing party. The skipper of the fishing boat saw them and made towards the unfortunate trio, and they were soon helped aboard and taken back to Beth with Don's dinghy in tow.

As soon as they were on board Beth, the first job was to get Lance's parents dried out and into some warm clothes. Lena took them down to her cabin, where she made them as comfortable as possible and did what she could to dry out their clothes. Meanwhile Don was drying out the outboard engine. Peter had started the compressor and with the airline blew out the water from the vital parts of the engine - it was the only outboard motor they had and was an essential part of Beth's equipment.

The colonel and his wife had almost dried out, the outboard had been put back together and was running and once more they climbed into the dinghy and this time, reached the jetty safely.

"I hope they don't think this incident is typical of what goes on aboard," Don remarked to Lena, on his return from the yacht club.

"I'm sure they wouldn't have let Lance stay if they had any worries about his safety," said Lena.

"It was an accident", said Don, "but it was partly my fault. I should have made sure that they were wearing life jackets and had them sitting amidships. If the bows had been higher out of the water we would have ridden that wave." Don let it go at that, as recriminations were not his style. Although Lance's mother lost her handbag and her presents, and both of them had had a nasty shock - the waters around Balboa are notoriously shark infested and they were in the water for around fifteen minutes, they did not blame anybody or make a fuss. It was treated fairly lightheartedly, once they were picked up.

The following day, 20th October, they prepared to leave and Don checked off all the things he had to do before sailing. The bills were settled, he had arranged with the Commonwealth Bank in Perth to have money waiting for him in Rarotonga, Beth's route had been given to the harbormaster, and all the other formalities had been attended to. Beth was ready for sea again.

"Puss, puss, where are you? Puss, puss, puss. Has anybody seen Biscuit?" Lena was looking for her cat.

"What a time to disappear, the pilot will be onboard any minute now," said Don. He was not sympathetic to Lena's loss - if he had had his way the cat would not have been onboard in the first place.

Biscuit, a great big tan colored cat, had been given to Lena in return for some work Don had done aboard a German freighter in Grenada. Don had expected cash for the work and the gift of the cat had only added insult to injury. He hated cats, and that particular animal, sensing his dislike, used to annoy him even further by doing his business in the wheelhouse. Lena had grown very fond of Biscuit and used to protect it from Don, who would have shot it given half a chance. But now Beth was about to leave and the cat was missing.

"Don, have you seen Biscuit?" Lena looked accusingly at her husband.

"I saw him this morning, he must be around somewhere. There's nowhere he could go apart from swimming ashore, and he wouldn't do that." Don was more interested in getting underway than looking for the cat. Beth was moored against a freighter away from the jetty, and he had a suspicion that the cat had been stolen by the Chinese crew of the freighter. He kept his suspicions to himself, however, while Lena searched Beth from top to bottom.

At 4.00pm the pilot came aboard and Lena was still looking for Biscuit. The engagement of the pilot to guide them out of the mooring was a local requirement and Don, under his direction, had to turn Beth.

"Astern, ahead, hard right rudder, astern, astern, full astern," shouted the pilot. Beth was still behaving erratically, not responding properly - the bolt in the propeller had not fixed the problem after all. They were turning under the direction of the pilot, and very close to the old freighter they had previously been moored against.

"Hard astern!" yelled the pilot, as Beth approached the freighter, bow on. Don turned the variable propeller control to astern and wound the engine up to full speed. Beth did not go astern; in fact, she increased her forward speed and rammed the freighter! The old trawler's bows made an enormous dent in the steel side of the ship, and her upper deck was showered in rust and paint flakes. Don had visions of large compensatory bills he would have to pay; but the crew of the freighter, who were leaning over the rail and watching, thought it was hilarious, and they cheered and laughed.

"Let's get the hell out of here," said the pilot. Beth by that time had responded to the control and was going astern.

The rest of the manoeuvre was carried out without incident and Beth headed towards the end of the jetty where the pilot would be landed. As he was leaving the boat he turned to Lena and asked about the cat.

"It's beautiful; a great big tan cat, like a small dog. Have you seen it?" said Lena. Her hopes had risen at the pilot's interest.

"No. I haven't seen it, but I can guess where it is now. You were moored against that freighter, and most of the crew is Chinese. Chinese are very partial to cat meat and I'd bet a week's salary that your cat is in the pot aboard the freighter," said the pilot.

Lena thought he took some delight in telling her that – almost as though he was getting his revenge for the embarrassment he had just been through. Lena and Jonathan were very sad at the loss of Biscuit and the thought of his untimely and undignified end, as they left the jetty. Beth headed into the Gulf of Panama, destination Esmereldas in Equador. The time was 5.10pm.

*****

Lena Goes Shopping
In A Canoe

On the 21st. October, Don watched the mounting sea with some apprehension. After almost a month in Balboa, he found the rough weather most uncomfortable. As usual, he was seasick and although he was not keeping a watch as such, tried to keep as busy as possible. There was plenty to do, and the more industrious he was, the better he could keep his mind off the nausea - by then so familiar to him. At 5.00pm the log recorded their position as 19" 20' west, 7" 17' north. They had traveled 95 miles from Balboa.

The entry had barely been logged when the engine started running easy. As soon as Don heard the note of the engine change he raced down to the engine room. The engine was fine and with no load on it, it was just ticking over. The trouble was with the propeller control again. Don went up to the wheelhouse and tried the variable pitch control - it was completely free and easy to turn. Something had broken or come adrift! The blades of the propeller were in the neutral position and Beth was losing steerage way.

It was not a job that could be left until daylight. They had been traveling parallel to the Colombian coast, about ten miles off shore when the breakdown occurred. With no power, Beth was at the mercy of the seas, which looked increasingly threatening and the coast line - what they could see of it, did not look inviting. What looked like a rocky shore coupled with an onshore wind gave an added urgency to fix the problem very quickly. Don and Peter worked frantically in the engine room to remove the steel decking and get at the propeller linkages. First the vertical drill had to be moved, then the deck plates, and finally the deck boards in the stern covering the stern gland and the variable pitch links. As soon as the last boards had been removed, Don could see the problem - the pitch of the propeller was controlled from the wheelhouse through two ¾ inch steel rods, to the propeller. Both of the rods were broken, and one showed signs of having been broken for some considerable time.

"No wonder she was playing up in the Canal and at Balboa," Peter said looking at the broken links. Don remembered vividly his frustration as he tried to go astern with the pilot aboard - he also recalled a bang and a severe jolt in mid-Atlantic that was never explained.

"We're going to have to arc weld a splint across those rods, Peter," said Don. "We haven't got a replacement for either of them. Get someone to give you a hand and fix up the welder, and I'll see if I can find something to weld across them." While Peter was getting the welder going, Don looked around the engine room for some steel he could use to repair the rods with. The best he could find were a couple of steel bolts, four inches long and ¾ inches in diameter. They would not make the most professional job but they would take the weld and be strong enough to complete the repair. It was going to be an awkward job, lying in the stern bilge trying to weld a heavy bolt on to the rod, with barely enough room to work and the sea throwing Beth around like so much flotsam.

It was no good standing there and thinking about it, the wind was blowing Beth nearer to the shore by the hour. Don crawled into the bilge space and wriggled himself down to a position where he could work, and Peter, who by this time had got the arc welder generator running, passed the welding leads down to him. Lying in the bilge in a pair of shorts, he fastened a bolt to the rod using two pairs of mole grips, and then he started welding. The smell of the bilges on top of his seasickness was not helping. He tried drinking a Coke, but could not hold it down long enough to get any enjoyment from it. Everything he touched was wet and made the shocks he was getting from the welder even worse. It was two hours of absolute torture before he had the first rod welded, but it was a good job and would not break again.

Lena, in between fetching cans of Coke for Don, had tried lying on her bunk but Beth was rolling up to 50 degrees at times and she was being thrown out as fast as she got in. It was impossible to stay in the bunk and she finished up on the deck of the cabin, praying that Don would soon have the engine running.

Beth was drifting nearer the coast with every minute, and by the time Don had made the first weld, the rocks were only five miles away and looking very formidable and menacing. By now an expert at welding in this most uncomfortable position, he started on the second rod, which was completed in half the time of the previous weld. Three hours after the linkage failure, the rods were repaired. Peter switched off the welder and tried the wheelhouse propeller control.

"It works a treat," shouted Don from the bilges. "Let's get the gear back and the engine started, my stomach can't stand any more of this rolling." It didn't take long to have the engine room decking and the rest of the equipment back in place, and the old Gardner engine was restarted and soon Beth was under way again. The violent rolling steadied and the crew who were not involved in the repair came out of the corners they had wedged themselves into. It had been a close call - they had drifted with the wind, far too close to the shore for comfort. They headed out to sea and safety. The time was 9.00pm.

Three days later Esmereldas was sighted. The journey from Panama had not been particularly pleasant, with big seas all the way and the weather, humid and overcast. The Caisleys had to get their sea legs again after their long stay in Balboa, and the violent reintroduction to a sailor's life had made them all very seasick.

The entrance to Esmereldas - according to Don's charts, was a little tricky and he was glad to meet some local fishermen just outside the harbour and get some information from them before entering. He stopped Beth alongside their boat and exchanged greetings. The crew told him they were just about ready to pack up for the day and would be going in to Esmereldas, and they offered to guide Beth in. Don gave the skipper a bottle of whisky and followed the fishing boat - which had to slow down in so that the old MFV was able to keep up. By 9.00pm on the 24th they were anchored in the harbour. The fishermen gave Don a bit of information about the harbour, telling him that it was a poor anchorage, so he ran out plenty of chain with the anchor.

It was dark by then - too late for the customs, and as everybody was weary from the journey, they wanted to do nothing except rest. A deck watch was set and they settled down for the night.

Around midnight, Lena, who had the deck watch with Len, came down to the cabin and asked Don if he would take a look up top.

"We're not sure what is going on," said Lena. "Either everybody is moving, or we are." Don rolled off his bunk and followed Lena to the upper deck.

They were moving alright - the anchor had dragged and Beth had drifted clear out of the harbour! When Don arrived on the deck, she was well outside the harbour, with her anchor and chain swinging uselessly underneath.

"Len, go and get Peter to help you get the anchor up". Raising the anchor was a two man job. "I'll get the engine started." Don knew he had to get back to an anchorage in the harbour, and this time it would be without the fishermen to guide him. It was dark and the tide was running fast against Beth as she slowly re-entered the harbour, making for the anchorage she had just left. When they reached the mooring, Don had to juggle with the propeller control to hold Beth against the tidal current while the anchor was dropped, and this time he put out every bit of chain in the locker.

The next morning, the yellow quarantine flag was raised but by this time, Don had no expectations that the customs officers would visit them - he intended to go ashore and present the necessary documents to the authorities as soon as he had had breakfast. Peter dropped the dinghy over the side and fitted the outboard motor, ready for the visit. About a half an hour later,

Don was getting into the dinghy with Peter to go ashore, and discovered the Seagull outboard motor was missing. It could not have fallen off, and the only explanation was that it had been stolen. Jonathan said he had seen some locals snooping around the boat while they were having breakfast, but didn't see what they were doing. Don was furious - they had only one outboard motor. The trip to the customs would have to be made rowing the dinghy and if the outboard was not recovered, a replacement would have to be purchased.

After a long and tiring row, Don reported to the customs and when the formalities were completed, went to see the harbour police to report the theft of the outboard. The official was indignant that Don could even have suspected the Esmereldans.

"No, it's not possible, the local people are hard working fishermen and completely trustworthy," said the policeman. "Your motor must have fallen off the dinghy. Go down and have a look on the bottom when you get back."

When Don got back to Beth, he put his diving gear on and had a look on the bottom under the boat: there was a faint chance, but the outboard was not there. Sometime later while talking to the crew of a freighter that was moored nearby, he mentioned the loss of the outboard.

"I'm not at all surprised," said one sailor. "We always post a 24 hour deck watch with a rifle here. The locals would steal the boat from under you if you gave them half a chance." That comment confirmed Don's suspicions that the Esmereldans were not to be trusted.

Following the theft of the Seagull, a replacement was purchased, a Mercury Twin that Don could ill afford. Apart from the cost, he had other misgivings about the new engine - it was temperamental and did not perform as well as the one that had been stolen, and besides, he had got to know the Seagull and all its habits. It was part of Beth, and no matter how good the replacement was, would never fully take its place.

The visit to Esmereldas was not going particularly well! The locals seemed intent on aggravating the crew of Beth at every possible opportunity, and on one occasion, Don was ready to take his rifle to them and had to be restrained by other members of the crew.

The anchorage in the harbour was a difficult one - Beth continually had to be moved. It was the same for all the boats in the harbour, which was at the mouth of the tidal River Esmareldas. The locals didn't appear to be worried much about the inconvenience, and would lift the anchor and sail back to the mooring every so often. Whilst the anchors were dragging, their boats would bump and jostle each other and it seemed to be the accepted thing. For the crew of Beth, living in between decks, being bumped by another boat was most disconcerting. It felt as though they were being rammed, with crockery being knocked out of its stowage, and pens sliding halfway across a page if someone happened to be writing a letter. One boat, having dragged her anchor, was alongside Beth and bumping her every two or three minutes. It was a boat about the same size as Beth, but scruffy and filthy, looking as though it had not been cleaned nor had a coat of paint in all its fifty years of service.

After about half an hour of the continual bumping, Don asked the skipper if he would move as Beth was holding the bottom at the time. The skipper and crew just laughed and waved their arms about, but did nothing. Don went back after several more minutes had elapsed and asked again, but got the same response. The third time he told the skipper if he did not move his boat, he would go over personally and knock out his anchor shackle pin! The bumping still continued, and by that time Don was so angry, he grabbed a hammer and pin to go over and carry out his threat. He jumped off Beth on to what he thought would be the foredeck of the offending boat, a distance of some six or seven feet. Unluckily for him, the chain locker hatch cover was off and he landed badly on the edge of the locker, taking the full force of the fall on his chest. Peter quickly jumped across to the other boat and helped his father out of the chain looker and back aboard Beth.

Don was coughing blood and in no fit state to do anything, but he wanted to get his rifle and finish what he had started. Wisely he was restrained and helped down to his cabin where Lena took a look at his chest. Apart from some abrasions, there was no apparent injury, but he was complaining of severe chest pains and Lena was worried that he may have suffered some internal injury.

"You ought to have an X-ray," she warned him.

"No bloody fear, I don't want any Equadorian witch doctor poking me about, that's all they would be here, witch doctors. Just strap my chest up Lena. It'll be OK in a couple of days."

Don's critical attitude towards the Esmereldans had been building since they arrived, but by this time he was not in a fit condition to do anything about it - an X-ray taken in the Marquesas Islands later confirmed he had broken three ribs in his chest.

"Tomorrow we'll fill up with fuel and water and go," Don said. He did not want to stay any longer than he had to. From Esmereldas, it would be a long time before Beth would stop anywhere where provisions could be obtained and so Lena prepared her shopping list and went ashore with Don. Beth was anchored about a mile offshore, and the trip in the dinghy, by then fitted with the new Mercury outboard motor, took only a few minutes. Once ashore, Lena went off on her own to do the shopping and Don went to make arrangements for fuel and water.

A couple of hours later, Lena - then heavily laden with two full shopping bags and a box of groceries, got on a bus to take her back to the jetty where Don had dropped her. The bus ride was less than comfortable: the rickety old bus was packed to capacity, and all the passengers had some package or basket they were carrying. Some even had animals! There were no windows in the bus, which was probably just as well considering the heat and the animals on board, and the dust from the dirt road came in choking clouds, enveloping the occupants. Fortunately, the trip was short and Lena was set down at the jetty with her shopping after a dusty ten minute ride. After waiting for and hour with no sign of Don, she made her own arrangements to get back to Beth. She hired a local man to paddle her out to the boat in his canoe, and with the shopping stacked in the centre of the flimsy craft, she settled herself in the bows.

The Esmereldan, seated in the stern, began the mile long journey out to Beth taking the shortest route, straight across deep water. Lena couldn't swim and became worried. She asked the canoeist to keep close inshore where the water was shallower and she felt safer, and as they traveled along, sitting in the stern with her arms folded across her bosom, she felt like some royal personage with her own personal slave to do her bidding. The Esmereldan then came to the point where he had to turn into deeper water to reach Beth. Lena still felt rather regal, but also very tense - she was thinking of the 14 fathoms of water under the fragile canoe, but it arrived alongside Beth without mishap and she was helped aboard with her groceries. Although It was a just a minor incident in a journey that had been crammed full of excitement, the shopping trip in a canoe would remain a pleasant memory for a long time. She wished at the time, that her mother and sisters could have seen her.

On November 1st, Don took on a full load of fuel, water and other provisions as the next port of call was to be in the Marquesas Islands. Between Equador and their destination lay the vast expanse of the Pacific Ocean, broken only by a group of volcanic outcrops some 540 miles away - the Galapagos Islands.

Early on the 2nd, he visited the harbour authorities for the last time, to get clearance and give his projected route and destination for the next stage of the journey. Don intended to sail to the Marquesas via the Galapagos Islands, but was more than surprised when he was told that on no account was he to go near the Galapagos Islands - a permit was required to land there and very few of these were issued. The penalty - if Beth was caught in the waters around the prohibited area was confiscation of the boat and equipment.

This was a major problem, although he didn't voice his concern to the Equadorian officials. The route he had plotted would take him by the islands and was strategic to his plans: he knew he had sufficient oil and food provisions to reach the Marquesas, but what he was less than sure about was the fresh water. Beth had a crew of nine now and water would have to be severely rationed if they could not obtain supplies at the Galapagos Islands. It was a problem that needed some thought, and Don mulled over it as he headed in the dingy back to Beth.

Don at that time, did not have a good word for any of the Esmereldans. He thought they were untrustworthy, and had deliberately made his life miserable during his stay - it had been impossible to make friends with them. But just before Beth's anchor was raised for the last time in Esmereldas, something happened to make him change his mind: a boat came over with a load of fruit for the Caisleys. It had come from one of the banana exporters, and although none of the crew had been involved with these people, they had heard about the stolen outboard and other incidents that had marred Beth's visit, and were trying to make amends. The bananas, egg plant, and other tropical fruits presented to the Caisleys were a nice gesture, and certainly did much to reverse Don's attitude toward the Esmereldans.

*****

Galapagos: The Ash Heap Of The Pacific

Beth sailed out of Esmereldas on the 2nd of November into a 13 to 22 knot wind, her course set for the Galapagos Islands. In spite of the warning, Don felt it was imperative to call at the furthermost island and try to obtain fresh water. It was not a matter of flouting the Ecuadorian law, but one where the safety of his family and crew was concerned. The navigation to the islands was not straight forward; the Humboldt Current - which runs up the west coast of Chile and Peru and turns back to the Pacific by the Galapagos, had to be taken into account. Peter had calculated that the island should be sighted sometime on the 6th. Navigation was still a little bit of a worry, but nothing compared to the problems that started to occur on the second day out of Esmareldas - as far as Don was concerned, and were to give him much more of a headache as Beth crossed the Pacific.

He had noticed the glass filter bowls in the fuel lines had changed color as soon as they had got underway. Then the engine coughed a few times and stopped - there was a blockage in the fuel lines causing an air lock at the engine. Don took the filters out and stripped and cleaned them; they were thick with black sludge. The following day, the same thing occurred; the fuel they had taken on at Esmereldas was filthy – and this was to cause problems all the way across the Pacific. Fortunately for Don, when he had installed the engine he had fitted extra filters in the fuel lines, and he was glad that he had taken the extra precaution. By the third day out he had resigned himself to the fact that filter cleaning was to be a daily ritual all the time there was Esmereldan fuel on board.

On the 6th of November, by Peter's reckoning, they should have sighted the Galapagos Islands. By noon that day, with no sighting, Don and Peter studied the charts for the area and it was the general consensus of opinion that they probably had not made sufficient allowance for the Humboldt Current and had come too far south. A course change of a few points to the north was made and from then on a sharp lookout for land was kept. By nightfall Don noticed that the masthead light was out, giving him another reason for calling at the islands.

The mast could be climbed and the light repaired with comparative safety in the shelter of an anchorage, but to attempt to climb the mast at sea was inviting trouble. On the 7th, Lena had posted herself on the roof of the wheelhouse, since if anybody could spot land it was her - she had earned the nickname of 'Hawkeye' during the voyage because of her keen eyesight. At mid-day Lena shouted down to Don:

"I can see something, it looks like a mountain."

Don grabbed his binoculars from the wheelhouse and peered in the direction that Lena had pointed. Yes, he could just see it - land off to starboard, about 40 to 45 miles away. Peter and his father pored over their charts again and did some calculations: it must be the largest island in the group, they thought. Isabella - or Albemarle as it is sometimes known, and the peak that Lena had sighted was the volcano Cerro Azul, rising to 5540 feet above sea level. It was precisely where they wanted to be. Beth was turned to starboard and headed for the coast, which was followed until a quiet bay providing good shelter was found and the anchor dropped. With the anchor down, the engine was stopped, but the noise had barely died away when a boat came around the headland towards them.

"Now we're for it, Peter," said Don. His heart came into his mouth as he had visions of an Equadorian gunboat arresting them and impounding Beth, then locking him and his family away in some grotty little prison.

The closer the boat came though, the less it looked like a gunboat. In fact, if anything, it was very much like Beth in many respects. It turned out to be just what it looked, a fishing boat, owned by Americans and doing exactly what Don had been warned not to do - poaching. The boat came alongside Beth and once she was anchored, the usual maritime courtesies were exchanged, and the crews visited each other's boats and swapped sea stories. The skipper of the American boat told Don he had plenty of fresh water aboard, but he was short of coffee. There was plenty of coffee aboard Beth but Don was worried that the fresh water he carried wouldn't be sufficient to last to the Marquesas Islands, so a deal was made - fresh water for coffee.

Beth was anchored in the bay for two days, during which time the masthead light and other necessary repairs were made. It was a very exciting visit to this most unique group of islands, some of which are uninhabited. Dubbed by Charles Darwin during the historic voyage of HMS Beagle, 'The ash heap of the Pacific', the islands are entirely volcanic in their origin - some craters are still active. It was here that Darwin found clues to his controversial theory of evolution.

After watching Don and the boys go ashore in the dinghy, now fitted with the powerful Mercury outboard motor, Lena decided to put on a lifejacket when it was her turn to go ashore. Up to then she had never worn one, except for the time she was towed to the beach in the Canary Islands. The speed that the dinghy was traveling with the new motor had Lena a little worried. The less powerful Seagull would have cruised at a much more leisurely and safer speed than the Mercury and to Lena it seemed that the dinghy was almost flying, with just the engine in the water.

Once ashore she enjoyed the visit, walking amongst the seals, birds and iguanas - all completely without fear of man. The family climbed the volcanic rocks to get a better look at the island and were totally stunned by what they saw. The view was completely unlike anything they had ever seen before - just a few stunted trees and rock after rugged rock, looking more like a lunar landscape than any earthly scene. Jonathan scrabbled around collecting pebbles and pieces of rock and shell, imagining himself to be an astronaut exploring some far distant planet.

Back aboard Beth, the boys fished off the side of the boat and found they did not even have to bait the hooks. The fish, about twelve to eighteen inches long, snapped at the hook and almost delivered themselves on board! Everybody would have liked to have stayed longer in the Galapagos Islands, but it was not possible - Beth should not have been there in the first place, and every hour they stayed increased the chance of detection by the Equadorians. They had accomplished what they had set out to do: repair the masthead light and fill up with fresh water. Now they must resume their journey across the Pacific - destination, the most northerly islands in French Polynesia.

Inwardly, Don was worrying about this next stage of the voyage. When Beth crossed the Atlantic, he had the whole coast of South America to aim at should there have been an error in the navigation. The Pacific crossing was different! The Marquesas were just a speck in the vast Pacific Ocean, 2000 miles away, and the slightest error would put them miles off course and into danger that he dared not contemplate. With characteristic stoicism, he banished the fears from his mind and got down to the task of plotting the course with Peter. They had crossed the Atlantic and made a good landfall with Peter's navigation: they would do so again in the Pacific.

At 7.00pm on the evening of the 9th, Beth left the bay on the island of Isabella and set a course of 269 degrees, running on the diesel engine. The following morning, Don raised as much sail as Beth carried and stopped the engine. The wind was fair and behind them but Beth was not making as good a speed as was expected of her. Several combinations of sail were tried, and eventually, with the main sail swung out to starboard and the gaff sail swung to port, she had what seemed to be the most effective area of sail.

With Beth under sail and the weather sunny and fine, Peter and Jonathan decided to make use of some of the balsa wood they had picked up in Esmereldas. They constructed a huge kite, using some of the six foot lengths of very light balsa. Some old pieces of canvas were tied to the framework which was then fitted with a tail, and a long length of nylon fishing line completed the kite. It was then released from the bows, feeding a little of the line at a time, until it was flying high above the waves, some hundred yards off the port side. The wind dropped and the kite dipped down and fell behind, so the boys followed it round, feeding the line around the stays until they were at the stern. The kite was losing height, so Peter wrapped a loop of the line around his hand, pulling it in a series of tugs, in an effort to raise it. His efforts were not successful and the kite took a sudden dive into the sea; however, with the drag of the water on the kite, the loop of nylon bit into his hand. Peter couldn't remove the line, which was trying to pull him overboard or cut through his hand, and he shouted for Jonathan to cut the line as he was being pulled further and further over the stern. The line, eventually severed, drifted off with the kite leaving Peter nursing his hand where the nylon had bitten into his flesh. It was a near thing - something they dare not tell their father, who had been asleep at the time of the incident.

Don found out anyway and decided to put their hands to more profitable labor while they were off watch.

There was a 20' X 18' tarpaulin on board, a relic from Don's trucking days - if only he had a boom, the tarpaulin could be used to increase the sail area. Then he remembered some timber he had been given by the crew of a Danish ship while they were in Balboa - Don would collect anything useful, and those pieces of timber were stored in the glory hole at the stern. The lengths were 7 feet long and 4"X2", but there was a fairly large quantity of them. The boom would have to be 20 feet long, and by binding the lengths together with steel and welding the straps, taking care to stagger the joins, a substantial boom could be made 20 feet long and 8"X4".

While Don was working on the boom, the rest of the crew were busy sewing ropes to the tarpaulin, ready for attaching to the boom. When this was completed, a large hook was attached to the centre and the tarpaulin fixed along its length. The making of that square sail took days to complete, but once it was hauled up the main mast using the stay sail block, it billowed out and filled. Two ropes either side of the bottom of the tarpaulin were secured to the deck and Beth took on the appearance of an oriental junk, with her one big square sail dwarfing the other conventional sails. With that unorthodox, but effective rigging, a competition was held to see which watch could make the best distance - Lena and Len held the record with 24 miles being traveled during a four hour watch.

Although the ship's log recorded nothing unusual during the Pacific crossing except for the occasional problems with lights and minor adjustments to the engine and sails etc, there were of course, a plethora of activities which were part of life at sea but did not rate a mention in the log. One such activity was to break the monotony of the middle and morning watches by singing through the list of top twenty pop songs. With Beth plodding along under sail or engine, the incessant swish of the propeller wash or flap of the sails was broken by the watch keepers trying to remember the latest pop songs, in order of popularity, and singing them through the silent hours.

Jonathan had a sense of humor which would either endear him to the other crew members, or rate a few harsh words - depending on what they were doing or how they were feeling at the time. During the many periods of rough weather that Beth encountered, he would put on the record of the Royal Marine band playing 'A life on the ocean wave' - to those whose stomachs were heaving with the motion of the sea, the strains of the band would probe every corner of the boat, mocking the afflicted. More than once, Jonathan almost found himself wearing the record player around his neck, rather than playing it!

For Lena, cooking and preparing the meals was something she had to relearn. Even the simple task of making a cup of cocoa could be somewhat of a complexity, and it was not only the heaving sea that caused the difficulties. Most culinary chores were made difficult by an insidious group of stowaways - weevils. Every powdered food substance; flour, cocoa, dried milk and even gravy powder had to be shaken through a sieve before use. Cockroaches were another problem, or nuisance. Although during Beth's refit the hull was scoured down to the bare wood and repainted, and the entire interior was similarly treated or replaced, these obnoxious pests still managed to remain aboard.

Life at sea aboard Beth was never dull whatever the weather conditions. During fine weather the off watch crew members would sit on the foredeck playing guitars and singing, if they were not required elsewhere, however, there was always some maintenance work to be attended to - either sails, rigging or engine. One activity that aroused everybody's interest was the daily sweepstake: that could be the total miles over a twenty four hour period, the mileage under sail alone during a four hour watch, or how many flying fish would land on deck during the night. Just about anything that had some uncertainty attached to it was gambled on!

Jonathan's diary throughout the voyage indicated many of the activities that were engaged in aboard Beth:

10/11/73: 'Got up at 7.30. It is very hot today. We put up all the sails today and we caught a small tuna fish this morning which we had for dinner.'

11/11/73: 'Caught another tuna today which we had for dinner. We put the mizzen topsail up today.'

Fishing from the stern was a constant pastime aboard, when the weather was favorable, and apart from the sport that fishing and chasing turtles provided, the tuna and other fish caught supplemented the diet and were always welcome on Lena's varied menus.

*****

A Feast of BBQ
Goat In The
Marquesas

On the morning of the 26th November after nineteen days at sea, Peter, who by this time was extremely confident with his navigation, announced that they were close to the Marquesas Islands and land should be sighted soon. Don could smell the land. The earthy, humid odor of lush tropical vegetation came faintly at first, contrasting with the tangy smell of the sea. At midday 'Hawkeye' sighted the tiny island of Ua-Huka - it was exactly where they had expected it to be, and close enough to make no difference to the time given by Peter.

Don felt very good about that landfall. His confidence in Peter's navigation had been vindicated, and all the worries about being lost at sea were now behind them. At 4.30pm he dropped the anchor in a small deserted bay on the island of Ua- Huka.

Jonathan's diary for 26/11/73 reads: ' *Did some schooling today and just as I was finished I heard a loud 'Land Ahoy' from Peter. After 19 days at sea we found out it was the*

Marquesas so we made very good navigation. Then we changed course for one of the islands where we anchored for the night.'

They were now in the South Sea Islands and naturally, after a nineteen day voyage, everyone wanted to go ashore. The beach looked inviting with lush green vegetation skirting coral sands, but the skipper had to be strict - he had no authority to land there. The customs, police and other authorities were on the islands of Hiva-0a and Nuka-Hiva, and it was to one of those islands he had to go first. It was a somewhat disgruntled crew that settled down for the night, waiting to be allowed ashore.

Beth was under way straight after breakfast next morning for the short trip to Nuka-Hiva, arriving before mid-day. The anchor was dropped in the bay of Taiohae and the quarantine flag raised, however, it was not the Customs that came out to Beth, but the local natives, in dugout canoes, and from experience Don knew he would have to go ashore and present himself to the authorities. He took Tom, the American who had joined them in Balboa, and together they went to see the chief of police who, according to Don's information, was the administrative officer for the islands. Once ashore, Tom annoyed Don by walking into a plantation - which was obviously fenced, and helping himself to the fruit growing there!

"Hey Tom, come out of there, that belongs to somebody," said Don. "Don't let's upset the local people before we start our visit by stealing their crops."

"This isn't stealing, they're God's own fruit." Tom picked a ripe paw-paw and proceeded to eat it.

"If that's the way you're going to behave, then you're on your own. I most certainly will not be responsible for, or condone, your actions," said Don.

Tom took umbrage at Don's reprimand, and Don was angered by his arrogance. He remembered from the books he had read before the voyage, the bloody history of these beautiful islands: once cannibals, the Marquesans had been shamefully treated by white men. From a population of 50,000 at the beginning of the nineteenth century, down to 20,000 by 1842, and to a mere 2,000 in 1926, their numbers had been decimated by murder and disease brought by the Spanish Conquistadors and others over the years. The islands, now administered by the French, are slowly starting to climb out of the decline in population with better medical and other facilities, and strict administration.

Don found the office where the authorities were located without difficulty, and presented the ships papers and the passports to the customs and police in Taioehae. His knowledge of French, from his trucking days, proved to be a useful asset in dealing with the French speaking officials, who were most friendly and helpful. The chief of police invited the Caisleys to his home for tea and was fascinated as they related their adventures on the voyage so far.

The invitation was of course, reciprocated, and Don and Lena entertained him on board Beth, putting on a meal that would have done credit to a first class restaurant with all the facilities. The exchange of visits were enjoyable occasions and the Caisleys learnt a lot about the islands and their inhabitants from the police chief. Don thought how easily these friendly people could be taken advantage of, but the chief assured him that a careful watch was kept on all visitors and he and his staff knew exactly what was going on and who to take action against, if necessary. The harbour in Taioehae had several expensive looking yachts moored there, and Don discovered that the Marquesans would feed the crews as long as they stayed. There were obviously some who were taking advantage of this generosity. Money was not an essential commodity in the islands, except for such items as fuel - which was expensive by comparison to what Don had been used to.

On the second day in Nuka Hiva, Lena took Jonathan ashore to do some shopping. They found three shops, one which sold meat; however, it was not like any other butcher's shop that Lena had ever seen. Meat was only available early on the morning that the butcher returned from a hunting trip, then the beef, goat and pork - depending on what the butcher had caught that day, was sold in the most unorthodox cuts.

Jonathan's diary for 28/11/73 read: *'I went ashore again today. We had a look for some shops. We found three and one was like Cranfield post office (Cranfield was the village in Bedfordshire where the Caisleys were living before the voyage), it had everything in it. Another thing we found out, the butcher goes hunting for their meat.'*

What Don did not realize was that there was now beginning a world wide crisis in the supply of fuel. Normally, he would have topped up his tanks to capacity, but with the Marquesan fuel oil priced at $25 per 50 gallon drum, took on only a part load. He had somewhere around 800 gallons on board, and as the next stage of the journey was much shorter than the last, considered it to be sufficient. He would completely fill his tanks in

Tahiti or Raratonga where hopefully, the price would be more reasonable - money was still a problem.

The chief of police had told them about other islands in the group and Don wanted to see at least one more on his way to Tahiti. Ua- Pou was only 30 miles away and would be a good starting point for the next leg of the journey. Before leaving he was asked by two Italians if he would take them to Tahiti, to which Don agreed, provided they could pay for their food and a little towards the running costs.

With these additional passengers, there were then eleven people aboard Beth, and the safety equipment would have been hard pressed in a real emergency. There was the eight man life raft and the dinghy, plus a rubber raft, also there were sufficient lifejackets - in a calm sea, adequate maybe, but the seas are not usually calm in an emergency! Don thought the sharks would have a good time, but then put such horrific thoughts from his mind. The Italians boarded and Beth was made ready for sea.

The visit to Nuka-Hiva had been idyllic: this rugged but lush green island was all that the Caisleys had hoped for in the South Pacific. The people were gregarious and friendly, and Don later recalled the family's thoughts - they would not have been opposed to staying in the Marquesas, had it been practical. It was a dream of course, and not feasible. They needed money to live on - in spite of the generosity of the islanders, and they could not have earned a living there. But the South Sea Islands are the place of dreams and it was natural that their thoughts would stray in that direction.

On the 5th of December, Beth left Nuka-Hiva and sailed for Ua-Pou, some 30 miles distant, arriving in the evening. If the greeting in Taiohae was friendly, then the way they were welcomed as they dropped anchor in Ua-Pou could only be described as overwhelming. Don had sailed around the island until he found a small bay, fringed with palm trees and edged with a grey sandy beach, and on a glassy blue sea Beth had glided to a stop and dropped anchor. Hardly had the hook hit the sandy bottom when the water was full of native dugout canoes - little copper skinned boys and girls, older men and women, all paddling out to greet the Caisleys, and before long, the deck of Beth was swarming with those dusky people, anxious to be friends. The younger children were especially inquisitive, and Jonathan's diary recalls: *'All the children came on board. All the grownups are very nice but the kids are a nuisance.'* The native children were as much at home in their dugout canoes as English kids on their tricycles, handling them with skill and agility.

It was so delightfully unexpected - the stuff of adventure stories, and it took the crew a while to settle down to more mundane duties. One of the children, a small boy, had told Don that his father had an outboard motor, just like the Mercury that Don had bought in Esmereldas. It would not go, and could Don fix it? Of course, he would be glad to take a look at it, and he promised he would go ashore and see it first thing in the morning. While Beth was in Nuka Hiva, Don had repaired a chain saw for one of the locals and had been paid for the work with two live chickens. Money was not an essential commodity there and he was only too pleased to be able to return the hospitality he and his family were being shown.

That evening, once the islanders had left, the family sat down to dinner. Beth seemed so quiet after the past two hours. The boys were planning the day ahead - they would go snorkeling for oysters and maybe find some pearls. Don would go ashore and have a look at the outboard motor as he had promised, and Lena was going to spend a lazy day on the beach. They were all eagerly looking forward to tomorrow as they settled down for the night. During the early hours of the following morning, Don was awakened by a sudden movement of the boat. There had not been a ripple on the water when they had anchored Beth, or when they turned in, but a stiff breeze had sprung up during the night and the anchor was dragging. With Peter and another member of the crew, Don raised the anchor and tried to find a more secure spot, still in the same bay.

The anchor had dragged so much over the past few weeks - it almost looked as though it was chromium plated as it came on board. With Beth once again secured and a deck watch set, they turned in for the second time that night. As Don lay on his bunk, the breeze was gently rocking the boat and the ropes clinked against the mast in rhythm with the water slurping at the hull. He thought the anchorage was not very secure, and the anchor would not hold Beth on the light sandy bottom against anything except the slightest breeze - a good wind could put them ashore or blow them out to sea. He had noticed a palm tree growing very close to the water's edge and it crossed his mind that the towing rope that Beth carried would reach the tree; with the anchor and the rope, Beth would be secure. He made a mental note to try the rope in the morning.

Straight after breakfast the following morning Peter and Jonathan took the end of the heavy manila rope ashore in the dingy and secured it to the palm tree, and with Beth now stern on to the beach and anchored from the bows, the rope was fastened to the stern post. Don was now satisfied that Beth would not move far and he went ashore, where he was met by the small boy who had asked him the previous evening about his father's outboard motor.

The boy took him to see his father who in fact was the husband of the chief of the island. The outboard did not present much of a problem - the main trouble was in the carburetors which were solid with years of accumulated muck. Once the 'carbs' were cleaned and reassembled, Don started the motor, and it ran as good as the day it was purchased, much to the delight of the chief and her husband.

To show their appreciation Don was invited to go hunting with them the next day. "Have you got any guns?" the chief asked him.

"I've got a .303 rifle, an air rifle and a pistol," said Don.

"Tch, tch, no we can't take the .303, it makes too much noise. The Police chief will hear us and we'll be in trouble. Bring the pistol and the air rifle," said the chief.

Don found out that although the islanders were allowed to hunt the wild pigs, goats and cattle on the island, they were strictly controlled as to how they hunted and the amount of cattle they could kill.

The next day Don went ashore with his rifle and pistol, wearing only shorts, a sweat shirt and rope-soled sandals. He had no food or water with him as the chief had told him he would not need any, so he thought that they would not be going far - how wrong he was! The party trudged through dense undergrowth for hours,

Don's sandals rapidly falling apart, and when they got hungry, the chief would just pick a paw-paw or some other fruit from a nearby tree and give it to Don. If they got thirsty, the chief or one of his party picked up a coconut and with an expert slash of his big knife, provided a drink. During the day they shot three goats and when they eventually arrived back at the beach, one goat was butchered and given to Don to take back to Beth.

"Come back tonight. You come with all your friends and we eat and have a good time," the chief told him as he prepared to get in the dinghy to return to the boat.

Back aboard, Don bathed his blistered feet and told Lena and the boys that they had been invited ashore. They had all heard stories from various people about the romantic islands in the South Pacific, but really did not know what to expect that evening, but from the invitation the chief had given him, Don was sure it was to be something of an occasion, so the Caisleys dressed for the event.

By sundown they were ready, and the dinghy took them ashore where they were met by a welcoming party of the chief, her husband and other members of the clan. From the beach they were taken to the schoolhouse, where a gargantuan feast had been laid out on trestles, and outside the islanders had prepared shallow ovens in the ground and a large wood fire. Over the fire on a spit, was one whole goat being barbecued. The ovens were covered with leaves and sand, and underneath were cooking, island style, the most delicious cuts of meat and other delicacies. As the ovens were opened up, the cooked meat was taken out and served on banana leaves and laid on the trestles in the schoolhouse.

Lena wondered how they could get any more food on the tables, which were by that time covered in shellfish, white fish - both cooked and raw, many varieties of fruit and vegetables, and meat dishes, all delightfully decorated with hibiscus blooms and other tropical flowers. Then the barbecued goat was brought in and laid across the backs of two chairs - it was a sumptuous feast and reminded the Caisleys of films they had seen with Dorothy Lamour and Bob Hope. The only thing out of place was the canned beer that some of the islanders were drinking, but that of course, did not detract from the excitement of the feast.

The barbecued goat was delicious and everything was so natural: no frozen food here - the meat and fish freshly caught and killed, and the fruit picked from the trees and straight to the table. Then there was the entertainment. The handsome copper colored Marquesans love music and they played their instruments - a sort of ukulele without a back, holding them against their stomachs, lifting them away from time to time to vary the pitch, and singing all the while.

When Don and his family had first planned the voyage, this was exactly the way they had imagined it would be in the islands. After more than six months of hardships and danger at sea, of worry and near disaster, here was the panacea, a utopia. There was no discord, no money, no economic problems and food in plenty. It was the essence of dreams and fantasies and the Caisleys enjoyed it while it lasted - they still had a long way to go.

*****

Christmas In Tahiti

The course to be set from Ua-Pou in the Marquesas Islands to Tahiti was not so straight forward as one might imagine from looking at the map. Between the Marquesas Islands and Tahiti lay a group of islands - the Tuamotos, low lying and in many cases, uncharted. Many of the islands are so low, in fact, that they cannot be picked up on radar screens. Most of the islands are little more than coral reefs, rising only a few feet above the surface, and present a hazard to even the most experienced navigators with every modern aid at their convenience. New atolls are constantly emerging from the sea, while others weather away and sink below the surface. The ocean currents are powerful and malevolent and have caused the sinking of a great number of ships. The area is known as the Pacific graveyard, and is probably responsible for more wrecks than any other. Add to these dangers, vicious cyclones during the months of December to March and you have the reason why Don wanted to steer clear of the Tuamotos Islands.

At 6.00pm on the evening of 8th December 1973, Beth sailed out into the South Pacific bound for Tahiti. On other occasions, once Beth was out of the harbour, her bows would be pointed at her destination and the course set to cover the journey in a straight line; now they were taking a roundabout route to miss the Tuamotos. It would be a good test of Peter's navigational skills, as by this time he was extremely proficient with the sextant and Don had no qualms about getting lost.

The foresail and topsail were set, and the mizzen and mizzen topsail as they left the Marquesas Islands bound for the 'Gem of the Pacific'. The weather was good and the crew sailed off in high spirits with fond memories of the Islands.

After a little over four days at sea and many course changes to detour around the Tuamotos Islands, land was sighted on the morning of the 13th. It was the island of Tetiaroa, one of the more northerly of the Society Islands. By noon the following day, Beth was approaching Tahiti, its green peaks looming out of the distance, embraced by a scurry of clouds. As the island began to take shape at their approach, Don called Papeete harbour control. Tahiti, like so many other South Sea Islands, is surrounded by a coral reef, and because of the navigational hazards on entering Papeete harbour it was necessary to obtain assistance of a pilot. Anxious to put to good use his knowledge of the French language, he requested the assistance of a pilot in French; however, Papeete harbour control answered in English, probably because their mastery of the English language was superior to Don's French! At 4.30pm a small pilot boat was sent out and the pilot told Don to follow them through the reef, and half an hour later Beth was anchored in Papeete lagoon.

If the Caisleys had expected this paradise to be silent except for the wind sighing through the swaying palms and the sweet singing of the Tahitians, they were mistaken. Papeete was alive with the sounds of engines

- motor cars, motorcycles, motor scooters and on the lagoon, motor boats, racing boats and outboard motors. Even the traditional outrigger canoes had engines fitted to them.

Many of these motors and engines would be silenced in the following days after the arrival of Beth. The effects of the world fuel crisis had reached Tahiti, Don discovered to his chagrin after he had gone through all the formalities with the authorities. There was no fuel available for Beth. It may be a few days, or a week, a month, or even longer. There was no end to the shortage in sight, he was told.

Don had sufficient fuel on board to take Beth to her next port of call, Raratonga in the Cook Islands, but ever cautious, he did not want to leave without full tanks. He had not completely filled his tanks in Nuka-Hiva because of the price, but in Tahiti there was no fuel to be had at any price. The Caisleys would have to remain in Papeete until fuel was available.

To most, such an enforced stay would be no hardship, one would suspect. To be stranded amongst such lush surroundings, tropical nights, wahines attending and garlanding the visitor with gardenia and frangipani blossoms was the essence of dreams. Truly, the Polynesian island is a paradise, but it costs money to stay there and each day Beth was in the lagoon Don's finances were dwindling away. Tahiti, unlike the Marquesas Islands, is a popular resort and easily accessible by air and sea. Consequently the cost of living for the tourist is very high, and so they had to economize and make the best of it. They had brought their own accommodation with them, so hotels would not be a problem. There was plenty of work to do about the boat and they settled down to enjoy their stay, doing most of the things that tourists do, without being either lavish or miserly. Don would review the situation every few days and act accordingly.

Lena and Jonathan with Australian family in Tahiti

It was a good opportunity to get some exercise ashore so Peter, Len, Lance and Oliver decided to take a hike around the island. Oliver was the only one of the four to have any camping equipment, but the weather was warm and it was not considered necessary to have sleeping bags, tents and the like. After rummaging around in the glory hole at the stern of Beth, they found an old tarpaulin that would serve as a groundsheet, and for supplies they took a few tins of condensed milk and some bread and biscuits.

The foursome set off to climb the mountain they had seen as Beth approached Tahiti. It was an invigorating climb, through lush tropical rain forest, and food was available wherever they looked, fruit growing wild on almost every other tree. At the top of the mountain they decided to camp for the night, and the sun was setting as they dumped their packs on the ground in a clearing surrounded by tall trees.

The weather changed dramatically with the sunset - as they looked down in the direction they had just climbed, the clouds seemed to roll in underneath them, obscuring the island. As the mist closed in, the temperature dropped, and from the warm sunshine of the day it became cold and clammy. Soon it began to rain. Oliver had erected his one man tent and was soon asleep, while Peter, Len and Lance huddled in their blankets and the old tarpaulin. Before long the rain had soaked through the blankets leaving the boys wet and shivering. Water was running down the mountainside and they moved the tarpaulin several times to get away from the mini rivers of rainwater that were forming - Len even left the groundsheet and tried to sleep standing up in the shelter of a tree! After a while it was apparent that wherever they moved, they were not going to avoid the water. The night passed slowly and dawn found them cold, wet and tired.

With the dawn, the sun shone and the heat of its rays soon began to warm the dejected group, however, Instead of turning back as they had discussed during the night, they decided to continue the hike.

Several days later they arrived back at the mooring, after hiking right around the island. They climbed back aboard the old trawler, tired, dirty and hungry after an expedition that had not cost them a penny, and they had enjoyed almost every minute of it.

Beth had been in Papeete a week, when the royal yacht Britannia arrived in the lagoon on the 21st. of December towing the fleet auxillary Blue Rover, which had been crippled by a serious fire in the engine room. It was quite obvious that the tanker at least, would be there for some time while repairs were carried out to make her seaworthy. Don put on his best whites and went over to the tanker to see if he could be of assistance and maybe earn a little money to help defray the expenses of his enforced stay in Papeete.

He found the first officer of the tanker and offered his services, but to no avail: no help was needed as the Blue Rover had all the hands on board necessary to repair the damage caused by the fire. The Caisleys were however, invited on board, and that invitation turned out to be the beginning of the best Christmas the family could ever remember. What had all the indications of a quiet, almost bleak festive season with Don worried about fuel and the mounting harbour fees was turned into one of joyous festivity. The Caisleys were made honorary members of the petty officers mess, and visits were exchanged between the crews of the Blue Rover and Beth.

Christmas day was spent aboard the fleet auxiliary and all the trappings of a traditional Christmas were enjoyed. A gargantuan spread of turkey and pork was followed by plum pudding, and there was every type of drink available, from beer to the most exotic liqueurs, but nobody misbehaved or became obnoxious through being drunk. It was a party to remember. The next day, the tables were reversed and Beth was the venue for a Boxing Day feast. Lena did them proud, calling an all her culinary skills to provide a meal fit for the occasion. The crew of the Blue Rover was used to good food and plenty of it. Lena provided home cooking from her diminutive galley, and it was enjoyed and appreciated.

With no end to the fuel crisis in sight, it looked as though Beth would be in Tahiti for some time, so it was a good opportunity to paint ship. Some of the crew of the Blue Rover came over to help and were soon busy with paint and brushes, while others helped to repair and replace ropes and rigging. During all this activity, Lena was busy in her galley, preparing meals to feed the hordes of hungry sailors.

In between the work and the visits to the Blue Rover, the family managed to have a look around Papeete and do some sightseeing.

Papeete, in spite of the noise and bustle of the city, is still a charming place to visit. About five miles from the city, on the road that completely encircles the island of Tahiti, is Point Venus. The Caisleys made a point of visiting this historic place, where the first known Europeans set foot on the island that later became known to seafarers and landlubbers alike, as 'paradise'.

It was there in 1767, that HMS Dolphin of the Royal Navy - commanded by Captain Samuel Wallis, anchored in Matavai Bay. Five days previous to landing on the black sandy beach, Captain Wallis had sighted the tall mountains of Tahiti, and followed the coast around the island looking for a safe anchorage. Imagine the surprise and delight of the 150 sailors aboard the 32 gun frigate - who had been at sea for eight months looking for 'Terra Australis Incognita' and were exhausted and smitten by scurvy, when they were welcomed by almost 500 canoes! The canoes were paddled by 4,000 athletic paddlers bearing gifts of fruit, coconuts and young pigs. That was not all the sailors saw: standing in the middle of each canoe was a beautiful Tahitian wahine, naked from the waist up, caressing her breasts and making inviting and provocative signs to the sailors.

Those same sailors - scruffy, scurvy ridden and hungry, who had been cooped up aboard the warship for eight months, with no female company and only their memories of what delights a beautiful girl could give, were then feasting their disbelieving eyes on five hundred half-naked and delectable young nymphs. It was little wonder that the sailors brought back stories to England of a 'paradise' in the South Sea Islands!

Lieutenant Cook - later Captain, followed two years later with an astronomer to observe the planet Venus as it crossed the sun on June 3rd 1769.

Twenty years later, Tahiti was one of the causes of the mutiny on the Bounty: the crew being angry at the harsh and pitiless discipline of the acrimonious Captain Bligh, and sad at leaving the carnal pleasures of Tahiti, mutinied three weeks after leaving Matavai Bay. The mutinous crew, led by Fletcher Christian, returned to Tahiti after setting Bligh and eighteen of his officers and men adrift in a boat near the Tongan Islands.

Don and his family watched in fascination a tradition that goes back long before Wallis, Cook or Bligh - old Tahitian women making crowns and garlands of gardenia and frangipani in the market place of Papeete town. Everywhere the rich perfume of tropical flowers pervaded the air, more especially in the evening when the incessant buzz of motor scooters had died away, along with its accompanying smell of petrol fumes.

Sitting on a black sand beach and watching the sunset decorate the horizon with shades of red, pink and orange while listening to the evening breeze sighing through the casuarina trees, Don thought of the country he had left - England, wrapped in the cold of winter and to him, an even worse situation - the Common Market. He had made his decision and was well on the way to achieving his goal, and his worries of the past were well behind him now. The beauty, peace and tranquility of the South Sea Islands had the magic to erase bad memories of the past and as the colors of the sunset gave way to the velvet blackness of the tropical night, they were washed from his mind. Once again, as in the Marquesas Islands, he found himself musing over the notion of settling permanently in the South Seas.

For him, the fuel crisis had passed. Don knew he would get fuel whatever the worldwide situation, but he did not know when. The crew of the Blue Rover had told him that as soon as repairs were completed, they would need to do a refueling exercise to check out the pumping equipment, and Beth could assist and be the subject for the exercise, getting her fuel tanks filled in the bargain.

But then something quite unexpected happened: on the 14th of January 1974, absolutely without warning or any idea that the fuel situation had changed, Don was informed by the French authorities that he could fill his tanks, and that he did, to capacity!

By this time everybody had settled into life in Papeete, and it would be a wrench to leave the delightful island - there were still places to visit, invitations which had been accepted, and a few little jobs still to be done aboard Beth. The Caisleys held a family conference to decide on when their departure date should be, and they decided to stay one more week. It would still be a wrench to leave Tahiti, but they wanted to continue their journey to Australia -there was still a long way to go, and shortage of funds would remain the major worry until the voyage was over.

Once the news that Beth would leave Tahiti on the 21st got to the crew of the Blue Rover, they instructed Don to bring a couple of empty tea chests over on his next visit. He loaded the chests in the dinghy and went over to the fleet auxillary tanker, whereupon the crew promptly filled them with everything that they would need at sea, from toilet rolls and soap to canned foods, and every subsequent visit until Beth sailed for the Cook Islands followed the same procedure - the crew filled two chests full to overflowing with provisions for Don to take back to Beth. However, the final visit was one to be remembered throughout the rest of the voyage for something other than the generosity of the Blue Rover's crew. The quartermaster told Don he had been cleaning out the cold room and had come across a quantity of eggs that had not been turned. Would he like them? Don, thinking he was talking of maybe two or three dozen eggs, said he would love them. To his utter astonishment, the dinghy was loaded with the two tea chests, one of which was full of eggs. Beth's crew ate eggs all the way to Raratonga and then across to New Zealand, where by that time they were thoroughly sick of the diet - even while they were alongside in Raratonga, Lena managed to sprinkle a few eggs on the menu!

On the 21st of January, the Caisleys went aboard the Blue Rover for the last time and made their farewells. Everybody on board had helped to make their visit a momentous one, so the goodbyes were somewhat protracted. Addresses were exchanged and promises to write were made - the Caisleys were to meet some of the crew again in Fremantle, Western Australia, where the family eventually settled. Some of the crew, then aboard another fleet auxillary - the Grey Rover, were in Fremantle for the Queen's visit, and Don and Lena were able to return the hospitality they had been shown in Tahiti.

*****

Don Renders A Service to the Queen

Beth sailed from Tahiti in the afternoon of the 21st of January 1974, after the most pleasant and memorable landfall of their voyage so far. The Caisleys still had 7,000 miles to go, and once out of the lagoon, the course was set for 262 degrees.

The first day out was spent tidying up around the boat, re-stowing food and provisions to make better use of the available space, and generally getting their sea legs again after a month ashore. On the second day out of Tahiti, the cruise ship Monterey steamed past Beth creaming a large bow wave, and on the decks, the passengers were waving and shouting as they left Beth behind in the graceful ship's frothy wake.

Day three and a mechanical failure occurred - the coupling from the engine to the main generator broke. Don stopped the engine and removed the faulty coupling, replacing it with a spare. All the spares that he carried, and was using, were proving that his caution was justified.

On the fourth day out, at mid-day, there was a disagreement over Beth's position. Peter wanted to stay on 262 degrees and Don thought the course should be changed. The old compass adjuster in Southampton had warned them that they would experience compass error south of the equator, and Don had this warning at the back of his mind as they approached the Cook Islands. Nothing had been done to the compass since his adjustment of nine months ago - basically because Don had not been able to find anybody to make the correction.

On this particular day, Peter had been unable to use the sextant because the sun had remained hidden behind clouds and the sea was quite heavy.

Don eventually took a DF radio bearing on Raratonga airport - aircraft beacons are not the best beacons for maritime navigation, and it indicated they should be steering not 262 degrees, but 310. Peter was not totally convinced, probably not realizing the magnitude of the compass error in the Southern Hemisphere, but Don said he was going to steer 310 degrees for two hours and see if the signal from the beacon got any louder. With the final word from the captain, Beth was turned to the new course and after an hour or so on 310 degrees, the signal was coming in loud and clear and increasing in strength: they were obviously headed in the right direction.

Don was at the helm, and the sea was rough with Beth rolling and pitching around, but making fair progress. His thoughts must have been on the beautiful wahines they had left behind in Papeete, for his mind certainly was not on the job in hand because he let the main gaff swing around. It came around with such a force that it jibbed and broke. It was a spar 20 feet long and six inches in diameter - quite a substantial boom holding the top of the mainsail, and it snapped in half like a rotten carrot. With the gaff useless and dangerous, the mainsail was hauled down and Beth continued ploughing through the heavy seas running on the engine and the mizzen sails. The gaff would have to be replaced in port.

At 5.00pm that day - while still steering 310 degrees, land was sighted dead ahead. Two hours later the Walker log read 676 miles, and it was then getting dark. The seas were becoming even heavier as they approached Avarua harbour, which like many Pacific island harbors has a rather narrow entrance through coral reefs. At the entrance to the lagoon was a post in the shape of a cross, on which was placed two lights, and farther into the harbour was another similar post with lights. For a safe approach through the dangerous reefs, the ship's head had to be lined up with the posts so that the lights on both posts appeared as one.

With the big seas throwing Beth around, Don found it difficult to see even one of the posts, as the boat was raised to the crest of a wave and then crashed in the trough of another, let alone see them both and line them up. The noise of the surf crashing over the reef did much to speed him to a decision. Once again, putting caution first, he turned away from the harbour and cruised around in the heavy seas until daylight, keeping the lights of Raratonga in sight. A daylight approach would allow him to enter the harbour with a good margin of safety.

Early on the morning of the 26th of January, Peter took Beth into Avarua harbour, through the narrow gap in the treacherous coral reef, and brought her alongside. At 0645hrs, the log recorded 'stop engine'. Don went ashore and attended to the usual formalities, and was told that he should not have been there at all - Beth had arrived at a very sensitive time for the Island. Raratonga was fervid with the impending visit of Queen Elizabeth, who was to open the new airport in three days time, and a radio communiqué had been broadcast to all ships in the area, warning them to keep clear of Raratonga until the Queen had left. Don had not received the radio broadcast and was blissfully unaware of the royal visit as he stepped ashore - they had already moored by the time they became aware of the visit, but as the Caisleys were British subjects and Beth a British registered ship, there was no real problem.

The islanders had bent all their efforts at decorating the place for the sovereign's visit, and Beth would have looked out of place had she not been similarly decorated. Don was a loyal British subject and made sure Beth was dressed for the occasion, with bunting from the stem, over the masts and down to the stern post. On the morning of the Queen's visit, Lena and the boys dressed in their finest and went along with the islanders to see the royal party at the new airport.

Jonathan's diary noted: *'January 28th. Raratonga. Got up at 7 30 am and had breakfast, then got ready to see the Queen arrive. When she got to the airport she waved to me.'* Princess Anne - apparently surprised at seeing English people in the welcoming party, came over and spoke to Lena, asking her questions about what had brought them to the Cook Islands. She seemed genuinely interested in Lena's story that they were on their way to Australia, and said she would have loved to visit Beth had there been an opportunity. Unfortunately, the royal schedule was planned months ahead, down to the last minute, and once the ceremony had been performed, they were flying straight out.

Meanwhile, Don had been asked to render a service to the royal party. The Cook Island authorities, knowing that Beth carried some diving equipment, had asked him and another diver to sit in a small boat, dressed in their diving gear, under the flight path of the royal plane in case - heaven forbid, there should be an accident. The facilities for security in Raratonga were almost nonexistent and the islanders were glad of any assistance they could get. Of course, the plane took off as scheduled with no complications, and the Queen, blissfully unaware of the excitement on the island that her visit had caused. Don returned to the harbour with his diver friend, their contribution to the royal visit over.

Don and Lena were invited by the local priest to call and see him. Lena accepted the invitation but could not persuade her husband to join her, as Don had an aversion to anything religious and would not even consider the visit. Lena took Jonathan and found the missionary most hospitable. They were shown over the church and around the grounds, and at the end of the visit Lena was asked to sign the visitor's book, where the priest had a record of all the visitors to the island.

As with every other port of call, the Caisleys were soon making friends with the locals. One very pressing need was for a boom for the mainsail, and as wood was not very plentiful on the island, it took quite a long search before something suitable was found. One of the friends they had made - an island trader named Bob Boyd, supplied Don with a beam from an old dismantled shed, and after planing the corners off and fitting it with the hardware from the broken boom, the replacement was fitted and would serve the purpose as well as the original spar.

Beth then had a telegraph pole as a mast, and a shed beam for a main gaff as well as a double decker bus engine and gearbox.

The Cook Islands, with basically the same attractions as Tahiti - both human and topographical, had at the time of Beth's visit attracted none of the tourists that Tahiti boasted of. The reasons mainly were accessibility and accommodation. The opening of the airport capable of handling jet aircraft had solved the access problem, but there were still no hotels of international standards. Raratonga was just a sleepy quiet town by comparison with the noisy bustle of Papeete, and Don and his family intended to enjoy every minute of their visit. They hired a small car and toured the tiny 26 square mile island.

Of particular interest to Don was the visit they paid to the island's power station where he saw two generators producing electricity, that were made by the company in England where he had spent his apprenticeship.

At Arai-te-tonga, just outside Avarua, they were shown the ceremonial stone on which prisoners brains were bashed out, the stone still stained with the blood of centuries. As they drove around the island, they were intrigued by the number of graves in front gardens, each covered by a metal roof - on each grave was placed a lantern, a water jug and a blanket. They never discovered the significance of the graves but thought it to be some religious tradition.

A surname that cropped up several times during their stay was Marsters. When Don enquired about the preponderance of the surname - which is not a common

English name, he was told the story of William Marsters. William was the farm hand from Gloucestershire in England, who settled on the island of Palmerston - the most northerly of the south group of Cook Islands, in 1862. With Marsters, were his Cook Islands wife and her sister. Understandably, after a while, the sister in law became lonely, so Marsters ordained himself a minister and married her - with his legal wife's consent of course. He then had two wives, and when wife number one became pregnant, another sister from a distant island – an expert in midwifery, came to assist at the birth. With the agreement of wives one and two, Marsters then married the other sister, making wife number three.

From all accounts they lived in complete harmony, producing a brood of copper skinned offspring with Anglo Saxon features, all speaking perfect English with the distinctive Gloucestershire accent. By 1880, Marsters had produced 60 children, and in 1946 the New Zealand Government estimated that the Marsters children and grandchildren numbered 2,508, plus more than 3,000 great grandchildren. In a population of 23,000 in 1973 for the whole of the Cook Islands, the Marsters offspring made up a goodly percentage. Many Cook Islanders migrate to New Zealand, and the name of Marsters can be found under multi entries in New Zealand telephone directories - William Marsters had certainly left his mark on the South Pacific!

One of the friends Don made in Avarua was the owner of one of the islands two pineapple trading boats. The chief engineer on this particular vessel had fallen sick with peritonitis, and Don was asked if he would like to take his place on a trip round the islands. After looking at the engine room, which Don described as the dirtiest and most dilapidated he had ever seen, he declined the offer. The engine was held together with baling wire and chewing gum, with oil running all over the place, and he was convinced if he took the chief engineer's place, he would never see his family again.

However, a replacement engineer was eventually found, and Don watched its progress with interest as the old pineapple trading boat sailed out of Avarua. Once clear of the coral reef, the two Crossley engines were opened up and emitted a pall of black oily smoke - just as Don expected they would. Long after the boat had disappeared over the horizon, the curtain of smoke could still be seen and Don was glad he had refused the offer to sail with her.

Just before leaving Raratonga, Don was approached by an ex-seaman enquiring about the possibility of a passage to New Zealand, and as always, with that type of request, the answer was yes, provided some help with the watch keeping was given and a little towards the cost of food was paid.

The man had not got a lot of money, but he had enough to pay for his food. He told Don that he had been brought to the Cook Islands on a stretcher as a terminal cancer patient. While there he had been a patient of Milton Bryck - the controversial healer, and had spent most of his money on the treatment. He was then ready to go home, cured.

If the man's story was true - and Don had no reason to doubt it, then there was something to Milton Bryck's claims of a cure for cancer. The ex-patient - though not a young man by any means, certainly looked fit enough

to withstand the voyage and keep sea watches. Don
would not have accepted him otherwise.

*****

Beth Loses Her Rudder

Peter and Don sat in the wheelhouse plotting the next stage of their journey. Originally, the course they had set out would have taken them to Suva in Fiji, making the first Australian landfall Brisbane. After the rough crossing from Tahiti, they decided to look for a better way. Don felt that the rough weather was a prelude to cyclones, and as they were right in the middle of the cyclone season, running to Fiji and Queensland would have been tempting fate. The alternative course was to sail south to New Zealand, and then to Australia. The charts they carried covered only the very north of the North Island of New Zealand, and any error of navigation would take them off their charts. They did, however, have pilot books covering the whole of the country, and after some discussion, they were confident they could make it with what they had.

On the 12th of February at 8.45am, Beth left the lush green island of Raratonga after refueling and taking on all the fresh water she could carry. Just before casting off, the islanders had hung festoons of flowers around the necks of everyone aboard. There is a delightful custom among Polynesian people, of throwing garlands of flowers from departing ships - if the flowers return to the shore after the ship has left, it means that the traveler will return.

Many garlands and flowers were thrown from Beth as she left the harbour, and Jonathan's diary bears the entry for February 11th: *'The custom when you leave is to throw a flower necklace overboard. If it floats back to shore you will be coming back some day. We hope ours floats back to the shore.'*

On the first day out, as soon as they had sailed through the reef, the weather became particularly unpleasant, and Beth was met by heavy seas as she left the relative calm of the lagoon. Mounting waves tossed the old trawler around, and as usual after a period ashore, everyone was seasick. When they were clear of the lagoon the Walker log was put out and Beth settled - if that is the right word, on a course of 252 degrees for Auckland, some 1700 miles away.

On the second day out, the log recorded the position at noon as 163' 22" W, 23' 38"S - this was an approximate position as the sky was overcast with occasional squalls, and there was no chance of a sextant observation. On day three the seas became even bigger with the green monster waves swelling grotesquely from the ocean floor and tossing Beth around like a cork in a maelstrom. For the boys in the foc'sle it was most unpleasant and even frightening at times - Beth would rear to the top of a wave, then crash down into the trough with a sickening thud that threatened to shake loose all the planks in her stout hull. The full force of those downward plunges was felt in the foc'sle mess, and for the man at the helm, looking ahead presented a frightening spectacle. An enormous wave would loom above the bows, and just when it seemed inevitable that tons of green water would come crashing on board, Beth would slowly climb to the top of the wave. When she was at the peak, the propeller - almost clear of the water, would thrash the air, vibrating along the length of its shaft until Don felt sure some damage would be done to the gearbox, or even the engine. Len moved out of the foc'sle - he had had enough of being thrown out of his bunk so he slept under the wardroom table.

By the fourth day, the weather had abated slightly and Don looked around the upper deck to see if they were still in one piece. He noticed one item missing. When Beth left Nuka-Hiva, she had on board two live chickens, given to Don in return for repairing a chain saw by one of the Marquesans, and they had been kept on the upper deck, secured to the deck with a string around one of their legs so that they could not fly away. They had been fed with table scraps, and mostly they would remain perched on the gunwale, clucking away and generally seeming to enjoy the sea voyage. Now there was only one, and the string that had secured the second chicken was hanging over the side. Don went to have a look to see what had happened: he pulled the string that was hanging over the side, and found that it was heavy. Then he looked over the stern towards the end of the string - there was the chicken, bedraggled and apparently dead, hanging within inches of the propeller. How long it had been that way nobody knew. The crew had all been far too preoccupied with the weather to take much notice of the poor old birds. Don hauled it aboard and was going to untie the string and commit the poor limp and sea sodden carcass to the deep; but while he was untying the unfortunate bird, he thought he noticed a faint shudder of one of its eyelids. Hardly perceptible, but he was sure he had seen it, and so he took the bird into the wheelhouse and laid it on the deck - the wheelhouse was immediately above the engine room, and the deck was always warm. With an old towel, he dried the chicken's feathers, but the bird showed no further signs of life: he was sure though, that he had seen an eyelid flicker. He asked Len to go to his to his cabin and fetch some brandy, because Don thought if there was any life at all in the bird, then brandy would revive it. Lena thought Don had finally flipped when she heard the request! He hardly ever drunk ashore let alone on board and at sea. The brandy was brought to the wheelhouse, and Don managed to open the chicken's beak sufficiently wide enough to be able to force a little of the fiery liquid down its throat. After a little while, and ever so slowly, the chicken opened one eye, and a little later, it wearily opened the other eye. With the warming effect of the brandy and the heat of the deck, it eventually dried out and recuperated sufficiently to be able to stand without assistance, and within a couple of hours it was back to normal, clucking around the wheelhouse as though nothing untoward had happened! Don then retied the string to it's leg and put it on the deck with the other bird, where it soon resumed its old position on the gunwale.

On the fifth day out of Raratonga, Peter killed the chickens for the pot. The two birds had almost become pets, and after the ordeal of the unfortunate hen that fell overboard, it didn't seem right to end their days this way. It had to be done though, as they were always meant to be eaten and they certainly would not have been allowed into New Zealand. After a few stiff tots of whisky, Peter was sufficiently inebriated to be able to perform the dastardly deed. Lena plucked and drew the birds and prepared them for the table, but nobody really enjoyed eating them. Apart from the fact that all the crew had grown used to seeing them perched on the gunwale and feeding them with table scraps, they were as tough as boot leather!

That same day there had been a minor problem with a slight tearing of the mainsail which was quickly repaired, but in the afternoon, the foresail sheet broke, and to repair it would have meant climbing the mainmast to feed the sheet through the block. The weather, after the lull of the day before, had then worsened, and it would have been dangerous to climb the mast and carry out the repair. The sail was hauled down and stowed, to be repaired when the weather improved or Beth reached port.

The weather did not improve, and Don kept looking at the barometer for signs of a change. He saw the pressure change from 1010 to 1022 over a very short period of time, and that gave rise to even more concern about the possibility of a hurricane. Throughout the next five days Beth battled through heavy weather, continually being pounded by the merciless waves, and every member of the crew who was not on watch, kept between decks and out of the weather - the upper deck was no place to be unless there was a great need or necessity to be there.

On the 22nd of February at 2.00am in the middle watch, mechanical failure caused Beth to gyrate even worse than the weather had managed to do. Len was at the helm when the wheel went slack. One minute he was wrestling with the helm that was trying the rip his arms from their sockets, the next minute he was holding a dead wheel that had was having no effect on the rudder! With no rudder control, the boat was being tossed around completely at the whim of wind and wave. Len called Don to the wheelhouse and he soon located the trouble: finding the fault was easy - fixing it was a different matter. The pulley, around which the chain controlling the rudder traveled, had broken loose from its mounting. It was mounted on the deck of the wheelhouse, and had been ripped out with the continual heavy weather pulling and snatching at the rudder.

It was possible to steer the boat from the stern by attaching a tiller to the top of the rudder post, but in the sort of conditions that Beth was experiencing, it would have been extremely hard work to operate, and the way the rudder was being snatched about, even dangerous.

Don set to work to make two plates that could be bolted to each other, through the deck of the wheelhouse. On the top plate would be mounted the pulley, and luckily amongst all the 'come in handy' bits that Don had aboard, was a box of very long bolts which would be suitable for mounting it. Meanwhile, the Walker log had been hauled in and the engine left running. With the engine running and no rudder control, Beth thumped on aimlessly, going in circles one minute, the next turning to port, and then to starboard. From the air, her wake must have looked like something out of a Will Hay movie! It was a relatively simple repair to do, and within a couple of hours the plates, with the pulley attached, were bolted to the deck and the rudder chain mounted. It was not a perfect job - there was still a lot of slack in the chain and that gave rise to a fair amount of free play on the helm. It did however, enable Beth to be steered from the wheel. A more permanent and professional repair would be made at the next port of call. After the

Walker log had been put back over the side and Beth settled back on course, Don crawled back in his bunk leaving Len to finish his watch at the helm. Later in the day he would be needed to help Peter with the navigation - Beth was not far from New Zealand now.

*****

South Of Auckland

Late in the evening of the 22nd of February, a light was briefly sighted through the murk. The weather was still very poor, with wind and squally conditions making visibility difficult. No positive identification was made but Don suspected that they were well south of Auckland, and off their charts. By the forenoon of the 23rd, the weather had not improved, but they were within sight of land. There were a number of small islands in the area, unidentifiable from Don's charts, so he decided to try and take a DF radio sight from Auckland airport. He tuned the radio to the beacons of both airports and took his sightings.

From the calculations he made, the airports appeared to be one hundred miles apart, and he knew that this was not so. Don assumed that the air navigation beacon signals were being reflected from the nearby hills and giving him an erroneous reading - he would have to contact somebody ashore using his transmitter, and get them to take a bearing on his transmission. He called Auckland ZLIQ, on 2I82.Khz, and the operator confirmed that Beth was indeed south of Auckland, and Don was advised to continue on his present course.

The weather conditions had not improved, with wind, rain and very heavy seas, and after eleven days of buffeting in the stormy Pacific, the Caisley's only thoughts were to get into a quiet harbour. Then, to the relief of everyone aboard, a large island was sighted - large that is, relative to the small islands they had seen so far. Don steered Beth towards the island with the aim of finding a sheltered bay where they could anchor for the night, before continuing on to Auckland. He sailed around the island until he had found a good anchorage protected from the fury of the Pacific, a small bay with a jetty. As Beth slowly entered the bay, the echo sounder was showing the bottom rising sharply and Don decided not to make for the jetty. He was not sure how much water there was, and to be on the safe side, anchored a little way out from the mooring.

As Beth's anchor was run out, a lighthouse on the island started sending out its warning beam: Peter was sure it was Cuvier Island at the entrance to Auckland harbour. The dinghy was put over the side and Peter and Lance went ashore, and as they tied up to the jetty the lighthouse keeper met them - Beth was expected. The lighthouse keeper had been listening to the communication between Beth and the shore station, and although he could not intrude on the conversation, knew that the boat would have to pass his way.

Peter and Lance returned to Beth with fresh milk and duck's eggs, and with the confirmation that it was indeed Cuvier Island. The fresh milk they brought back was the first they had seen since Tahiti, as in Raratonga fresh milk was not available. Lena made a pot of tea while Peter and Lance told the rest of the news. Don intended to stay overnight only at the anchorage, but there was time enough to exchange visits between the lighthouse and Beth. The keeper was shown over Beth while Don and the boys were conducted around the lighthouse.

At 10.00am the next morning, Beth left the shelter of Cuvier Island and sailed the 62 miles to Auckland, and by 7.00pm in the evening she was tied up alongside Marsden Wharf. Jonathan's diary records: *'Lots of people came and looked around our boat today and dad went ashore to see the customs.'*

Certainly the arrival of Beth in Auckland aroused a lot of interest and curiosity.

Once the formalities with the customs and other authorities had been attended to, the family went ashore to the Flying Angel where they picked up a whole bunch of mail that had been following them around. The weather in Auckland was fine and sunny, and it was good to be able to walk on firm ground. The damage they had sustained en route from Raratonga could then be repaired, ready for the rest of the voyage.

A steady stream of people came to visit and ask questions, and some looked at Beth and shook their heads in disbelief when they discovered that prior to the voyage the Caisleys had had no seagoing experience. A reporter from the New Zealand Herald interviewed the family, and wrote that Don and Lena were in two minds whether to stay in Auckland or carry on to Perth - the hospitality the family had been shown in Auckland had certainly prompted some discussion on the subject, and Peter even found himself a job on one of the boats there.

Jonathan had a slight accident while the boat was tied up at Marsden Wharf, which required a trip to the local hospital. His diary says: *'Went fishing today and caught a couple*

224

of fish. At about 12 midday Peter called me for dinner and on the way back I was trailing my fishing line behind me and somehow the hook got in front of me and I trod on it and got a hook in my toe. A man in a car picked me and drove me down to the boat and called mum and dad. Mum came down to the hospital to have it taken out. When they got it out they put it in an envelope and gave it back to me.'

While Beth was in Auckland, the two Americans left her - Lance, whose parents Don had tipped in the sea at Balboa, and Oliver. Don was loath to see Lance go as he had turned out to be a good seaman. Oliver, or Olive as Don called him because he had long hair like a lady, he was not so sure about. Oliver had suddenly decided, halfway across the Pacific, that he was going to be a vegetarian, and that had of course, completely thrown Lena's catering arrangements into confusion. With the Spartan facilities at her disposal, she could provide good, wholesome and varied meals, but for catering to fads she was not equipped. Oliver also brought aboard a motor cycle which had been stowed in the compartment above the propeller shaft, and as Don was aggravated more and more by 'Olive's' fads and weird habits, he became convinced in his own mind that the motor cycle had caused the compass error which had resulted in the navigation problems approaching Raratonga and New Zealand.

With the departure of Lance and Oliver, Don looked for another crewman, which was not difficult: this particular aspect of the voyage had been done so many times by then, that it had become almost as routine as clearing customs when Beth entered port. A New Zealander was taken on as crew, and Don also took on an American couple as passengers.

The next stop was to be Whangarei, just a few miles north of Auckland, and the manager from the Flying Angel missions to seamen had asked if he could go that far with Beth. He had heard so much about the voyage the Caisleys were making from other staff members around the world that Beth had visited, and it was an opportunity not to be missed. He intended to do a little fishing on the way. It was a request that was easily accommodated. The Caisleys had been treated very well by the mission and its staff in every port where they were represented, and Don was only too glad to have the opportunity to return some of that hospitality, and show the family's appreciation.

Early on the morning of March 11th, Beth left Marsden Wharf in Auckland. The sea was calm and the sun was shining; a good day for a cruise. By 9.00am she was off Rangitoto Island, and Don hoisted the sails and put the Walker log over the side. The man from the Flying Angel had got his fishing tackle ready to start fishing as soon as the deck was clear, and for the next six or seven hours, Beth cruised leisurely northwards. The Caisleys were enjoying the sunshine and the calm sea, and the man from the Flying Angel was completely engrossed in his fishing. By late afternoon they were off Little Barrier Island, and Don found a sheltered cove on the lee side of the island and dropped anchor.

The American couple were not at all happy - they had been seasick most of the way as Beth was no luxury cruiser and rolled considerably, even in calm conditions. On top of her nausea, the lady felt even worse when she went to the toilet: she got the valves mixed up and put the head in reverse, causing a minor flood - this was a fairly common occurrence when a new crew member used the toilet and Don was always prepared for a flood on the boat. It did not however, do anything to endear that particular lady to Beth.

Jonathan's entry for the day reads: *'Got up early this morning cleaned the brasses and we left at 8.30. The sea is not rough. We anchored off Little Barrier Island and we put the boat in the water and towed Ernie behind us on his surf board. After that we all went for a swim. When we were getting the dinghy out, one of the blocks from under the seats fell out and I had to dive in and get it.*

Just as I got out we saw a shark around the area where I was swimming so I was very lucky. '

At 6.30am the following morning, the anchor was raised and Beth continued on to Whangarei.

Whangarei is a good way inland, and Don was reminded of the Panama Canal as they approached, with a large expanse of water, islands dotted about, and posts marking the safe channel. By 2.30pm Beth was tied up alongside the fertilizer wharf in Whangarei. The American couple decided to cut their passage short and left once the boat was alongside - their complaint was that the sea had been too rough and they had been seasick. Actually the sea had been very kind, with barely a ripple on it! Don and Lena wondered how they would have felt had they taken passage on Beth from Raratonga to Auckland; however, the Caisleys were by this time hardened sailors, and used to the violent motion of Beth.

Beth stayed in Whangarei for a couple of days and Don did a couple of jobs around the boat, but anxious to reach his destination, sailed at 1.00pm on the 15th, through the twelve miles of Royal Passage and out into Bream Bay by 3.00pm. Two hours later Beth was past the Hen and Chickens Islands and off Bream Head, and the course set for 300 degrees. As they passed Poor Knights Islands to starboard, Don noted that the barometer was dropping, indicating the approach of rough weather. At 10pm and 51 miles from Whangarei, Beth was off Cape Brett and the barometer was down to 997 millibars.

On the second day out of Whangarei, they left New Zealand coastal waters at North Cape. The barometer was still falling and had got down to 992mb. A tanker traveling in the opposite direction about a mile away, was having waves continually break over its fore deck; but Beth's decks were still dry, even though she was being tossed around in the heavy seas. By 2.00pm on the third day, they had traveled 278 miles from Whangarei and were in the Tasman Sea - the wind was fierce, whipping up big seas and the first casualty was the mainsail, which ripped and had to be hauled down. Don noted in the log: 'very rough sea.'

That night as Lena made her way to the upper deck to do the middle watch, an incident occurred that she will never forget. The seas were mountainous, and Beth was plunging around like something tormented. As Lena opened the hatch to get to the upper deck, rain and wind driven sea spray whipped at her face, causing her to duck for cover momentarily. The wind was screaming through the rigging and Lena hooked her harness around her waist - as soon as she was out on the upper deck the harness would have to be clipped to the lifeline Don had rigged. Before she had time to secure the harness to the lifeline, a gust of wind whipped her off her feet and blew her along the deck towards the stern!

Was this to be the end of the voyage for Lena - being washed overboard in the middle of the night? It had happened so quickly. Lena uttered a short scream as she was swept along the deck, but the sound was lost in the raging of the wind and was not heard by any of the crew. As the wind blew her past the wheelhouse, she managed to grab a rope and haul herself to safety. She took over the helm wet, cold and still shivering from the ordeal.

Sometime during the forenoon, the foresail sheet broke and by noon that day they had come 430 miles from Whangarei. The heavy clouds had completely obscured the sun, and there was no chance of a sextant observation in those conditions. By dead reckoning, Peter approximated Beth's position as l68' 00"E 308' 48" S.

On the fifth day the barometer stopped its downward plunge and steadied, and then it began to rise. By noon it read 1002 millibars and the weather started showing definite signs of improvement: the wind had dropped and the waves had spent most of their fury. As the day wore on, Don started repairing the broken sheets and sails - a sure sign that the sea had abated. A sextant observation fixed Beth's position as 164' 11"E; 33' 51"S and the log read 586 miles from the last port of call.

The padre at the Flying Angel in Auckland had recommended Eden in New South Wales as the first Australian landfall for the Caisleys. He told Don it was a beautiful spot with a natural harbour, a good point to aim at, and so that was where Beth was headed. The weather by then had calmed down considerably, and on the sixth day out, Don had completed repairs to the foresail sheets and had the foresail rigged. At 1.00pm on day seven, all the sheets and sails had been repaired and they were under full sail again. That day with all the canvas up, Beth made 147 miles.

*****

Beth Reaches Eden

On the tenth day out from Whangarei, on a course of 305 degrees, the noon watch keeper sighted land – it was Australia, they had made it!

The first sighting was of Green Cape lighthouse at the entrance to Disaster Bay, and just 17 miles from Eden. The Caisley family rushed to the rail to take their first look at Australia, and amid the excitement Don steered Beth into Twofold Bay. The time was 3.00pm on the 24th of March 1974 when Beth moored alongside the tug 'Sydney Cove', in Eden - they had come 1385 miles from Whangarei, and a total of 14140 miles from Southampton in England.

It was a momentous occasion for Don, Lena, Peter and Jonathan: after ten months, they had finally arrived on the largest island in the world. Although their journey was far from complete, this landfall in New South Wales was the signal for a celebration. Jonathan wrote in his diary the day before arrival: *'March 23. We should get to Eden, Australia tomorrow and are all getting excited and nobody got much sleep because we all have our eyes peeled'*. The next day he wrote: *'March 24. Tied up against the tug Sydney Cove and as soon as we got there the cook gave us about 2lb of steak.'*

The gift of steak that Jonathan mentioned in his diary was initially given to him to use as bait for fishing; however, when his mother saw it she was rendered almost speechless - for the last ten days nobody aboard Beth had eaten fresh meat. The thought of Jonathan fishing with best beef steak was too much!

"You're not going to give him that to fish with, surely? It makes my mouth water just to look at it," she said to the cook on the tug.

"Let him have it. I'll make you a steak sandwich," the cook said, waving Lena's objections aside. Jonathan continued fishing and the cook, as good as his word, made a tray of steak sandwiches for the crew of Beth, the like of which Lena had never seen before. Each sandwich had at least half a pound of meat in it.

"If this is the way people live in Australia, I think I can quickly get used to it," said Lena as she bit into a very large steak sandwich.

The last twenty five days at sea from Raratonga in the Cook Islands to Eden in New South Wales, had taken their toll on Beth and the crew. For the crew, just to step ashore and feel something solid underfoot was enough to raise their spirits. But the old MFV - although built for the stormy northern seas, needed some serious attention - she had to be hauled out of the water for an inspection of the hull and given a scrape and antifouling. Barnacles, mussels and other clinging sea creatures normally cling to the surface of rocks, but when they attach themselves to the hulls of boats it is a major job to remove them. Even though Beth's hull was scraped in Balboa just six months before, the build up was causing a drag which increased fuel consumption.

After a rest, the Caisleys were very anxious to get ashore and do a bit of sight seeing, and find out a little more about the country they intended to settle in.

When Don left England, he had never heard of Eden except in the biblical sense. It had been on the Flying Angel padre's recommendation that he had made this small fishing port his first Australian landfall, and he was pleased that he did. As the Caisley family looked around the town of Eden, visited the museum and read some of the books written about Twofold Bay and the once thriving whaling industry, it occurred to Don that it was a strange coincidence that had brought Beth, an ex-North Sea fishing trawler, here, because Eden was a town so many fishermen from the same area had made their home over the years.

In the museum the family visited, they saw the skeleton of the last of the killer whales that had given the town a distinction unique in the world. For almost a hundred years, a pack of killer whales was used to hunt other whales and drive them into Twofold Bay, where they were harpooned and caught by the whalers. One family, the Davidsons, were so reliant on the incredible pack of killers that on the death of Tom - the whale now preserved in the museum, they went out of business because they had then lost their main asset. That team of killer whales acted for the whalers as a well trained dog does for the drover, and their story is as fascinating as it is incredible.

In Eden during the whaling season, the sound of someone calling 'Rusho, Rusho' would have an electrifying effect on the whole community. Men left their beer as they rushed from the bars, children left their lessons and housewives left their chores as they all raced to vantage points around the cliffs to watch the whales chase. The killers would drive their quarry within range of the whalers and when close enough, the unfortunate whale would be harpooned. Then came the most exciting part, as far as the cliff top watchers were concerned: the harpooned whale would race off in a frenzy and at high speed, towing the whaler's boat by the line attached to the harpoon. With a bow wave foaming, the boat would be pulled until the headsman could get an opportunity to lance the whale and deal it a death blow. Once the lance had struck, the whale would mill around in circles for about a half a mile or so before dying. It would then be cut loose, marked with a buoy, and allowed to sink to the bottom. The dead whale sinking would signal the pack of killers to claim their prize - they would follow the victim down, tearing out the tongue and gorging on the lips and other delicate parts of the carcass. After a few days on the bottom, the carcass would generate sufficient gases inside it to float it to the surface, where it could be towed to the processing factory.

This fantastic procedure was carried on year after year, with the same pack of killer whales returning to Twofold Bay to work with whaling boats, always driving their quarry into Twofold Bay where the unfortunate victim could be harpooned. Even at night the killers would signal the whalers by flopping and splashing about close to the whaling station, and then lead the boats out to where other the killers of the pack would be harassing a whale.

Tom was the leader of the pack and always had been, for as long as any of the whalers could remember. Other pack members had names like Old Ben, Hooky, Humpy, Stranger and Jackson, and were all individuals recognized

Sunday Mirror April 21ˢᵗ 1974

by the whalers. The pack gradually dwindled down until only Tom was left, then one morning his body was found washed up in a cove in Twofold Bay.

As Don and his family viewed Tom's skeleton in the museum, he tried to picture the scene in Twofold Bay, almost 50 years ago. The Caisleys were fascinated by the story of the whales, and were assured by the local people of its authenticity.

While Beth was in Eden, Don decided to see if he could do anything about the gearbox, which had taken a terrible pounding in the rough seas. Beth had traveled over 14,000 miles, and during that time he had noticed - or thought he had, a change in the sound, indicating signs of stress. The gearbox was giving 300 rpm at the propeller, and Don wanted to see if he could use another gear other than first and maybe get a few more revolutions from the propeller.

On April 6th, Beth was taken out of the water for scraping, antifouling and a hull inspection. While she was on the slip, Don took the opportunity to cut an inch and a half from the tip of each propeller blade - his idea was that a slightly smaller propeller would turn faster and he could use second gear. He was concerned that the 14,000 miles they had traveled in first gear had taken its toll, and it might be about to break, leaving Beth without power. In Southampton when the engine and gearbox had been fitted, second gear had been tried, but it lacked power and the revolutions of the propeller died off. By shortening the blades he hoped to rectify the problem.

When Beth came off the slip and back into the water, the modification to the propeller had been completed and Don took her out into the bay to give her a trial run. He had invited some of the friends he had made whilst in Eden, for the trip. The customs officer and other friends of the family came aboard for a tour around the bay and a demonstration of Beth - they didn't go far, just a few hours out to the headland and back, but while they were out, Don slipped the engine into second gear to see how his modifications held up. The engine was still a little underpowered in that gear, but it did run. The very fact that he could use second gear gave him a lot more confidence that if something should happen to the first gear during the remainder of the voyage, he had a reserve. In the event, first gear held up throughout the remainder of the voyage and second gear was never used.

Jonathan had a very good reason to remember Eden: he attended the local school for a few days during Beth's visit, and It was the first time he had been to school in almost a year. On Monday the 8th of April, 1974, he found himself the centre of attention. How he handled the laudation and admiration of his Australian contemporaries one can only speculate, but on the Wednesday of his four day period at school in Eden, he conducted his school friends on a guided tour of Beth. His diary for the period reads: *'April .7. All working very hard, I might be going to school tomorrow. Went to school on the 8th, 9th, 10th, 11th. On the 10th I took most of school out today. They all came to look at the boat. They said it was great.'*

At 4.00am on the 15th of April, Beth sailed out of Twofold Bay. The New Zealander from Auckland had left the crew in Eden - his only purpose in joining was to get to Australia, and he was replaced by an Australian, Rod Shultz. Three hours later they were off Green Cape and as Gabo Island was passed, the course was changed to take Beth into the Bass Strait. Leaving Point Hicks astern and heading directly into the strait, Don was a little apprehensive of what the next twenty four hours would bring.

Bass Strait has a reputation second only to the Bermuda Triangle for mysterious happenings and disappearances: apart from the many ships and planes that have sailed into the area, and then oblivion without leaving a trace, there have been many sightings of strange and eerie lights. For almost forty years, scientists and astronomers have been trying to solve the mysteries of the unidentified lights and UFO sightings. There has been no shortage of theories, with many people believing that in Bass Strait there is an underwater base for extra terrestrial craft. One factor which mysteriously links the disappearances, is that no SOS messages or mayday signals have been received from any of the ships or planes lost in the area. That must indicate that whatever misfortune has befallen the craft, it has happened with such speed so as not to give the crew time to call for help. Add to this the psychic side of the area and the strait's reputation for savage weather conditions and it is little wonder that this corridor between Tasmania and the Australian mainland holds fears even for the most experienced.

Apprehensive of what the weather would be like, rather than the psychic phenomena attributed to the Bass Strait, Don steered towards the oil and gas fields. The weather could not have been more pleasant, and the sea was dead calm and flat. It was so calm in fact, as to be almost uncanny. Don's worries moved from the weather to other stories he had heard, but always a pragmatist, he quickly dismissed the fears. He would need to see some concrete evidence of the mystery before he would attach much importance to it.

Cliffy Island light was sighted and passed, round Wilson's Promontory, and before dawn on the 17th they were off Cape Schanck with the Port Lonsdale light in sight by 6.00am. Abreast of the Port Lonsdale light, Beth turned and entered Port Phillip Bay through the Lonsdale rip, and two hours later she was tied up alongside the life boat station at Queenscliff.

The water was a bit shallow at the mooring and Don did not want to be sitting on the bottom at low tide, leaning against the jetty or, even worse, leaning away from it. Beth required at least eleven feet of water – a fact that Don was ever conscious of after the frightening experience at Balboa. He had noticed a creek, away from the life boat station, and walked around to have a look.

He found a local fisherman who told him of the conditions regarding depth etc, and helped him pilot Beth into the creek. Soon they were alongside in Queenscliff, and ready to go ashore.

During the short stay in Queenscliff, the Caisleys made friends with the locals and did a little shopping and sightseeing in Geelong and Melbourne. Jonathan was taken out one day by some of the local fishermen, and came back with a bag full of prawns and other fish, which provided a delicious meal for the crew. Another incident during Beth's stay, involved an ex-member of the crew who had left Beth in Trinidad. Somebody came aboard the day before Beth was due to leave Queenscliff and brought a copy of the Sunday Mirror newspaper in which was an article headed: "Fears grow for six on yacht". Len Platt, the bus driver cum-seaman, had gone to Brisbane after leaving Beth in Port of Spain, Trinidad, and had been waiting there for the boat to arrive. Unknown to him, Don had changed his plans in Raratonga, and sailed to Australia via New Zealand.

The newspaper report stated that Len Platt had left Beth in Barbados, when in fact she did not go to Barbados at all. It also stated that Beth's first stop was to be Lisbon, but it turned out to be Oporto.

The inference to the reader was that Beth was aiming at Lisbon but made a landfall in Oporto due to navigational error, whereas in actuality, although the navigation was still a bit primitive in that early part of the voyage, the landfall in Oporto had always been planned. Len Platt had told the newspaper reporter that they had been sailing for Barbados when Beth left Las Palmas, but if he had bothered to acquaint himself with the facts, he would have known that on the advice of the Norwegian skipper, Don was making for Trinidad, approaching it from a southerly direction in order to keep clear of possible hurricane activity.

Len Platt was convinced Beth would never reach Australia, and had told the reporter so; but of course, Beth had been in Australia for almost a month at the time of the report.

Don and his family read the article about themselves with considerable amusement - they all remembered Len Platt threatening to leave the boat every time a bit of rough weather was encountered in the Atlantic.

*****

Near Disaster On Ruby Rock

The day following the newspaper report, Beth left Queenscliff. Because of the Lonsdale rip, Don had to wait for the tide to be right before leaving Port Phillip Bay, and at 12.45pm Beth left Queenscliff – in Don's words 'like a cork out of a champagne bottle'. It was the fastest Beth had moved since she left Lisbon.

By 1.00pm they were out into the Southern Ocean bound for Portland, and at 8.00pm that evening with the Walker log reading 51 miles, they were sailing past Cape Patton, heading towards Apollo Bay.

There were now six people making up the crew, and the watches were arranged so that Lena and Len Fleming took the afternoon watch and the middle watch, Peter and Jonathan had the forenoon watch while, Don and Rod took the dog watches and the morning watch.

Early on the morning of the 23rd of April, a light was sighted. Don thought it could be Warnambool, but was not sure due to the rain and poor visibility. Two hours later they were approaching Griffiths Island, off Port Fairy, and at 2.15pm Lena – who had the afternoon watch with Len, took the helm to pilot Beth into Portland. Less than an hour later Lena had Beth alongside after a masterly bit of seamanship.

It was ANZAC day, and once again the Caisleys were made welcome by the locals.

Portland is a pleasant town and has a beautiful harbour, but Don and his family didn't intend to stay there long. This was to be the last port before Albany in Western Australia, so fuel and water were taken aboard for the 1,500 miles or so across the Great Australian Bight. At mid-day on the 25th of April, Beth was fuelled, provisioned and ready to leave on the penultimate leg of her long voyage. Len let go the forward mooring rope and Peter slipped the stern rope, while Jonathan in the engine room hit the starter button and ran up the engine.

Beth started to move away from the jetty when Peter yelled "Stop. Stop. Cut the engine!" Don in the wheelhouse immediately pulled the stop, and killed the diesel. Beth was moving forward very slowly as Don raced from the wheelhouse to see what the problem was. Peter pointed to a dinghy tied up just astern of Beth.

"We've somehow snagged the mooring line to this dinghy," he told his father. Don peered over the stern and saw the dinghy almost under the slight overhang of the counter.

"I'll get my gear on and go down and take a look," he said, and went to the locker and got out his diving gear - it was always ready, with the tanks full for such an emergency. Once under Beth, he could see that the dinghy had been carelessly tied up, using a very long mooring line: the rope had sunk under Beth and once her propeller started turning, had been picked up and was wrapped around the propeller - another couple of revolutions would have dragged the dinghy down to be smashed up by the big propeller blades. Don came to the surface and asked Peter to knock the propeller out of gear, then he went down again and turned the big prop by hand, unwinding the dinghy's mooring rope.

By 12.30pm he was back on board and Beth was under way, and fifteen minutes later the sails were raised and they were passing Lawrence Rocks. Beth thumped on - the old Gardner bus engine had not missed a beat throughout the voyage. They were making a steady seven knots, and the crew were all talking about what they would do when they finally reached Perth. Keeping well inshore, they rounded Cape Sir William Grant, then Cape Nelson, across Bridgewater Bay, and into Discovery Bay. A course had been set to Port Macdonnell and then to Kangaroo Island. They should be passing Port Macdonnell around 7.00pm in the evening.

The afternoon sun flashed across the calm surface as Beth ploughed a furrow across Discovery Bay. The watch changed at 4.00pm and Don took the wheel from Lena. Following the usual procedure when taking over the watch, he checked the depth: 45 fathoms, plenty of water under the boat, nothing to worry about. He made a course change of five degrees to the north, to run closer to the shore. Twilight came and went quickly. The moon shone out of a dark sky and the surface of the sea reflected back a myriad glittering stars. An hour or so later Don took another depth reading: ten fathoms shallower this time, but still a good depth. At 6.00pm Lena came up to the wheelhouse with a tray of tea for the watch keepers. Don was sitting on the big variable pitch control wheel and steering with his feet while Rod was leaning on the chart table. Lena placed the tea on the chart table and handed Don and Rod a mug each. As they were drinking their tea, the time was passed in idle chatter, reminiscing about the voyage and journey's end. There was no need to stand at the helm - in fact, if the truth be known, various factors had combined to make them complacent, even a little smug. The sea was mirror calm and they were nearing the end of the voyage.

Just before the watch changed, Lena, looking out of the wheelhouse, pointed towards the shore.

"What's that white line over there, Don?" Don turned on his unorthodox seat, and as he did so a wave hit Beth's port side, rolling her to starboard till her gunwales were almost awash. It was no normal roll! Beth was being pushed, as if by a giant hand, further and further to starboard.

Lena grabbed a rail to stop herself from falling, however she did not cry out - after almost a year at sea she was used to the unexpected. But she was scared, and so was Don. He could not get off the control wheel because the list was so great it forced him down. There was no bump and where previously the sea had been so calm, they were now in white water, the sea boiling and frothing around them. They were at least ten miles from the South Australian shore - or should have been, and Beth was spinning like a top, as though she were on the top of a revolving wave. Don shut down the engine and switched on the echo sounder. He looked at the compass, and that was spinning too. All around the boat was a maelstrom of seething water, but they were miles off the coast, or so he thought.

"What the hell is going on?" said Peter as he rushed into the wheelhouse. He looked at the compass which was still erratic, and then at the charts. Stabbing the chart with his finger, he yelled above the noise of the surf: "We're over that bloody reef. How the hell did we get here? Steer out to sea!"

That was much easier said than done - which way was the open sea? The boat had been spinning, the compass was still erratic, and they had no night sight because of all the lights burning on Beth.

The first priority was to take a visual bearing as the echo sounder showed no water under the boat. All the lights were turned off and their eyes gradually got used to the moonlight. Peter had by this time picked up a hand compass, which steadied much quicker than the main compass. Don quickly restarted the engine, and now that their eyes were accustomed to the night, they could see a line of surf behind them - Beth had just sailed right across the top of a submerged reef! With the hand compass, Peter steered a course southwards, and soon they were heading away from what was almost disaster. By the time the watch had changed they were sailing seawards, the echo sounder still going. They had watched the graph showing 1 - 2 - 3 - 4 - 5 fathoms under Beth, with bated breath, and it was only when the graph showed 40 fathoms they began to breathe a little more easily. Peter and Jonathan had the watch and were sailing on a new course of 320 degrees.

Everybody on board was well and truly shaken by the event. By the time they were in deeper, safer water, the enormity of the situation they had been in hit them like an ice cold shower. Very little was said for a while, then they all began talking at once. It soon became clear what had happened: they had ignored one of the basic rules of seamanship - always check with each other before making course changes, and always make sure that the new watch is aware of any incident that happened during the previous watch. Peter had made a course correction of five degrees north that would have just cleared the reef during the afternoon watch, however, Don had altered course by five degrees north during the first dog watch, without realizing Peter had made the same change. The combination of the two northerly changes had put them over the reef and almost ended in disaster.

The reef they almost came to grief on, known as Ruby Rocks - just off Port Macdonnell, where Victoria ends and South Australia starts, has claimed many ships. Had they foundered, they would have had a lot of company down there.

*****

Family Reunion In Albany

From the time of the near catastrophe, Don insisted that the depth readings would be taken every half hour, and logged. By the end of Peter and Jonathan's watch, Beth had logged 76 miles from Portland and they were past Cape Northumberland. During the next watch fog closed in and they were using the echo sounder for navigation, following the 100 fathom mark to Kangaroo Island. When the morning watch came up, it was still foggy and by 8.00am the Walker log showed they had traveled 129 miles from Portland. The echo sounder had been checked every half hour and then showed 65 fathoms. Throughout the forenoon watch the depth of water gradually decreased, and at 11.30am it was down to 24 fathoms. The sea fog had not cleared and by 1.00pm Don had to reduce speed. An hour later a further reduction in speed was made, and at 3.30pm, Peter gave their approximate position as 'off Margaret Brock Reef'. They had come 182 miles from Portland. During the afternoon of the 26th, the fog lifted and they could see the coastline. By the following midday Kangaroo Island could be seen, and just after mid-day a boat came alongside - it was the Lady Buick. The skipper did not come aboard, but he and Don swapped addresses and promised to write, then the Lady Buick turned back to Kangaroo Island after the skipper had wished the Caisleys luck, and promised to radio back to Portland and give the harbour authorities Beth's position.

By 3.00pm Cape du Couedic lighthouse was sighted, and an hour later they were past the Casuarina Islets and starting across the Great Australian Bight - the sea was calm and the sea fog had completely cleared. There were very few other ships in the area, and soon they were out of sight of land.

The following day Beth made good progress on a calm sea and in brilliant sunshine, but on day five out of Portland they ran into the weather that the Bight is notorious for - heavy squalls and a big sea. On Peter's noon sight, he charted Beth's position as 131' 22"E, 35' 28"S, and they had covered 588 miles. By 3.00pm that day, the weather had deteriorated even further and the sea was breaking over the deck - the weather had to be very severe before Beth's decks got wet. The first casualty of the weather were the navigation lights: they were fed from a junction box at the foot of the main mast, and the salt water had got into the box. Don cleaned out the corrosive salt and dried the box, and then he packed it with plasticine to seal it from the weather - the navigation lights were back on, but for how long? If there was the slightest trace of salt in the box, it would very quickly corrode the terminals and tomorrow or the next day, the box would have to be stripped again.

There were few mechanical failures on their journey across the Bight but the weather had turned really foul: as each succeeding day dawned, the sea seemed to increase in its ferocity. By the evening of the 4th of May, with no sextant observations being taken for some time, Peter estimated that they should be off Albany. Don could see lights and several small islands through the squalls, but it was dark and he was reluctant to take Beth in to a strange port at night, so he decided to cruise around until daylight. His idea was to head Beth into the weather and run the engine in opposition to the wind so that the boat was hovering. With a hand-held wind gauge, he had measured the wind velocity, and it showed it was blowing about force seven: the idea to make Beth 'hover' did not quite work as expected. As the night wore on, Beth was being blown further and further away from what Don thought was Albany, and by morning, although they were still within sight of land, it was not Albany that they could see as Beth was headed for the coast.

Don, along with everybody else on board wanted more than anything else to get out of the storm. By 7.50am the anchor was dropped in a bay, thought to be Bremmer Bay. At least they were out of the worst of the weather. All that day and night they remained at anchor in the bay, while the storm raged in the Southern Ocean. During the day Don took a DF sighting to try and establish their correct position: the only station he could pick up was Perth, but the bearing he obtained from the sight indicated that the anchorage was not Bremmer, as was first thought, but Dillon Bay.

Lena meanwhile was making the most of the relative calm of the anchorage, whatever it was called, as during the past few days she had been unable to bake in her tiny galley - whatever she put in the oven would come sliding out as Beth performed her antics in the rough water. One minute Beth would be climbing to the crest of a wave, and then she would hover at the peak with her big propeller vibrating throughout her hull, to come crashing down into the trough. Occasionally the waves would hit her broadside, and she would roll, often as much as 45 degrees, and the gyrations of the boat were playing havoc with Lena's baking. She was used to baking nine loaves of bread, twice a week. They would be placed, three at a time, in the tiny oven after being left to rise in the engine room where it was always warm. Now she set to work baking bread and cakes, and doing the numerous jobs around the galley that she had been prevented from doing because of the rough weather.

The following morning Don raised the anchor to sail round to Bremmer Bay. There were two reasons for his making this unscheduled call: one was because according to his charts Bremmer offered a far better anchorage than the place where Beth had been sheltering - the storm was still raging. But the main reason was communication: there were no facilities in Dillon Bay, and his relations in Perth would be wondering and worrying what had happened to Beth. In Bremmer Bay was a township of the same name where he could make a telephone call to tell his relations that Beth had been delayed because of the weather.

Beth sailed out of Dillon Bay, and once out of the protection of the anchorage, the boat reared into the teeth of the gale. Although Bremmer Bay was 'just round the corner' from Dillon Bay, it took a full four hours to reach it, fighting every yard of the way against wind and wave. Immediately they reached the bay the anchor was dropped, but the shelter afforded was not very good. Don raised the anchor again and sailed around the bay looking for a more sheltered position, and when the anchor was finally dropped, they were in a beautifully flat calm area, almost like a lagoon. Beth was completely out of the wind and there was barely a ripple on the surface - the water was so clear that the bottom could be seen.

Looking towards the shore they saw a car, traveling on what appeared to be a road. Peter put the dinghy over the side and went ashore, and soon he was back with milk and some other provisions, and information about the area. Don and Lena then went ashore, and were picked up on the road by a Mrs Walstead who was on her way to see her husband who was shearing sheep some distance away. The Walsteads owned a property in the area, and made the Caisleys welcome, inviting them home for a meal.

Beth stayed in Bremmer Bay several days, and the crew made many friends there. Don made the telephone call to his sister in Perth, and arranged that she and her husband would drive down to Albany and meet them there: in order to arrive at Albany in daylight, Beth sailed from Bremmer Bay just before midnight. By 4.00pm the next day, after an uneventful cruise through relatively calm water, Beth was sailing past Breaksea Island and into King George Sound. They passed the old whaling station to port, and an hour later were tied up alongside the grain wharf.

As Beth was being secured alongside, a man asked Don where he had come from. The accent of the man was familiar to Don and he said: "I can certainly tell where you come from. You're a Yorkshire man!"

"No. I'm an Australian now." said the man. He showed Don where to go for the customs and other formalities that had to be attended to before their stay could be authorized. When all the procedures had been completed, Don moved Beth and tied up alongside the town jetty for the rest of their stay in Albany.

As had been the pattern throughout the voyage, the Caisleys were soon making friends ashore. One lady asked Don if he would like a bath. To the landlubber, a most unusual offer, but to yachtsmen and people who travel long distances in small boats, a most tempting and welcome proposal! To be able to relax in a hot steaming bath after days, or even weeks, of 'cat's lick' washes from a small hand basin, would be as well received as drought breaking rain to an outback farmer. The offer was gratefully accepted, and Myrna and Keith Blythe entertained Don and his family with a bath and a barbecue at their home. They were yachting people themselves, and knew how much the opportunity to really 'wash off the salt' would be appreciated.

Late the following evening Don's family arrived in Albany. There was a joyous reunion, especially with his mother: she had said goodbye to them all in Falmouth, England, and although she had not voiced her fears, was sure she would never see Don, Lena and the boys again. Throughout that night and the next day, they were talking and relating their experiences, asking questions, and generally catching up on a year of news. It was a momentous occasion, a family reunion with a tired bunch of Caisleys and incredulous relatives. Nobody went to bed for two days: they just talked and talked, being revived by endless cups of tea, and for Don, cans of 'Coke'.

One other essential visit they had to make in Albany was of course, to The Flying Angel Missions to Seamen. Wherever in the world Beth had been, if the Flying Angel was represented there, Don and his family had visited them - they held the mission in the highest esteem for the courteous and hospitable reception they had been given throughout their travels. Don and Lena invited Tess and Tony Gadd of the Albany Flying Angel, to visit Beth, and thanked them most sincerely.

The voyage was still not quite finished, however, Australia is a big country, and Albany is a long way from Fremantle - Beth's final destination. There were still a few days sailing out of the Southern Ocean and into the Indian Ocean, before they could plant their feet on terra firma and stay there.

*****

"The Damn Bloody Voyage Is over"

Beth left Albany during the morning of the 14th of May. Don had taken on two passengers for the trip to Fremantle, Jeremy and Joanne, his sister's children. It was to be a big adventure for them. By 10.30am they had cleared the port, and an hour later the deck log records 'Flinders Pen', and at 11.45am the Walker log went in. Looking at the log which is only a rough deck log - the main log was not completed after Queenscliff, it becomes apparent that a sense of euphoria had enveloped Don and his family. The last few days they had spent at sea had been somewhat less than comfortable, but the reunion with the family had put all past trauma from their minds. That last stage of the voyage was just the tidying up, putting the finishing touches to an outstanding achievement.

As it happened, the last few hundred miles were not marred by any serious weather or untoward incidents. The sea was fairly boisterous, but the Caisleys were well used to that by now and were not the least troubled by it. Beth's passengers however, were certainly not accustomed to the violent motion as the old trawler ploughed into the Indian Ocean. They were very seasick, and spent most of the time lying down and wishing they were somewhere else!

On the evening of the 16th of May, Beth arrived off Rottnest Island. It was getting dark, and once again Don was not too happy about approaching a strange harbour at night. The lights of the island and Fremantle - with the glare of Perth beyond, were confusing. Don could not positively identify any of the lights or beacons he saw, from his book of lights. There were so many bright and different colored lights that the area looked like a gigantic fairground.

He decided to cruise around the island very slowly, and anchor until daylight. At 4.00am on the 17th the anchor was dropped, and as Don wanted all the lights on to show that they were at anchor, the back-up generator set was run up. When daylight came he could see that he had anchored just 600yds from the entrance to Fishermans Harbour. At 8.00am Don instructed, 'weigh anchor' - probably for the last time, and sailed the short distance into the harbour. He was fortunate to notice a spare berth as he entered, and quickly had Beth tied up alongside.

The captain shut off the engine and made one last entry in the log: "17-5-74. The damn bloody voyage is finished."

The voyage was not quite complete, however, Don still had to see the customs and the immigration authorities. He had been through the routine in a dozen or more countries - it was always a nuisance, to stand there while an official fussed over the passports, the vaccination certificates, the ship's manifest and the various other bits and pieces that are necessary before one can enter a country. This time it had a different twist to it - the Caisleys were not visiting, as they had done in other ports: they were coming ashore for good.

Len Flemming and the Caisley family shortly after coming ashore for the last time

Once Don had Beth tied up alongside in Fishermans Harbour, he raised the yellow Q flag, as he had done on so many other occasions. The customs officials came out to Beth and quickly went through the declaration that Don had made, including the firearms that Beth carried, and when they were told that the Caisleys intended to settle in Perth, they informed the immigration authorities. Beth arrived in Fremantle on a Friday, however, the immigration people were not available until the following Monday morning.

When the officer eventually came aboard, the problems started. For Don and his family the procedure was reasonably straightforward: they were British citizens, had valid passports, and had relations already in Australia. For Rod Shultz it was not a problem - he was an Australian anyway. But for Len Fleming, there was a big embarrassing problem: from the immigration officer's attitude, Don would have been better had he brought in Bubonic Plague or Foot and Mouth disease, rather than a black man! The immigration officer, with a broad Scots accent and obviously a migrant himself at some stage in the past, would not allow Len to leave the boat - not only would he not allow him ashore, but his attitude indicated that he had some personal feelings about colored people.

The attitude of the immigration officer did not endear him to the Caisleys, who had grown to respect the tall Grenadian over the past nine months. He had stuck with Beth through the good and the bad times, never complaining and always willing to do more than his share of the shipboard duties. Don had expected that there could be a problem on arrival in Australia, and had taken the precaution to see the Australian Consul in Balboa, before they sailed. His response had not indicated that the problems would be insurmountable, nor had the authorities in Eden shown that Len would be a problem, and therefore Don had not worried unduly.

It was not long before the media - particularly the television, picked up the story and invited Don to be interviewed on the subject.

Len Flemming finally settled in Australia and married. Seen here with his first child

He accepted the invitation and put his views over in a pithy and succinct manner. The interview may not have endeared some people to him in his new country, but he was not going to let a friend down when he needed him most. Eventually Len was allowed into Australia, on a temporary basis for three months while his case was reviewed by the Immigration Dept. in Canberra.

In the interview that Don gave to the television in Perth, he alleged that the only reason Len Flemming – who incidentally had a British passport, was not to be allowed into Australia was because he was black. A spokesman for the Immigration Dept. later denied the allegation and said Len Flemming was refused permission to sign off Beth in accordance with normal procedures applicable to crews of foreign vessels.

Beth in 1983 in need of some TLC!

With all the customs and immigration formalities out of the way - for the time being at least in the case of Len Fleming, Don started looking for somewhere to live. Money would again be a problem - at least initially, until he could sell the boat, as the total Caisley assets were tied up in Beth. Apart from the boat, Don had no more than A$250 when he came ashore in Fremantle. When the voyage was planned originally, he had estimated that he would have sufficient money left to place a deposit on a house in Perth. The trip had proved to be far more expensive than he had imagined, but it was worth it - an experience of a lifetime, and he still had the boat to sell.

There were plenty of potential buyers with cash, but they posed a dilemma for Don. The boat, if sold, was subject to import duty, and that would have been crippling - he needed every cent he could get to purchase a house and buy furniture and other essentials to start his new life in Australia. The deal he finally shook hands on was most bizarre, and one he would never have guessed at when he first purchased the old trawler from Lars Eric Ellinson.

The buyer naturally engaged a marine surveyor to look over Beth, and after his report the deal was settled. Don received a check for an amount sufficient to place as deposit on a house, a caravan, a Land Rover, television set, washing machine and a big bag of fruit together with several other small items of household use. It was indeed a very strange transaction, but it did set the Caisley family up and enable them to be independent, and have somewhere to live while they earned a living.

What has happened to them and Beth, from the time they arrived in Fremantle until this story was written?

Don and his family now live in a quiet suburb of Perth, and have become Australian citizens. They will always retain fond memories of Beth and the voyage they made in her.

Beth has not fared quite as well as the Caisleys, however. After Don transferred the title of ownership, the new owner changed her name back to 'Nordhaven', and then for a number of years - and after several owners, she was neglected. Once the pride and joy of Don and his family, she lay at her mooring forlorn and forgotten until the 9th of November 1980, when she quietly sank to the bottom in a place called Freshwater Bay near Perth.

Subsequently, the old trawler was given by the owner to Colin Clarke, if he could raise her, and eight weeks after she sank, Colin managed to get her to the surface and pumped her dry.

At the time of writing, the hull - for that is all that is left of Beth, now nicknamed 'Clarke's Ark' by the locals, after spending a few weeks on the slip is now in Fremantle harbour undergoing a major refit. The Caisleys have made several nostalgic visits to Beth since she was refloated.

Standing in what was once the engine room, and which now contains only the end of the propeller shaft and part of the variable pitch propeller control rods, Don pointed out to me the place where he had welded the bolts across the linkage in Equador. On the upper deck - now clear of any superstructure except for the stump of the main mast, he showed me the slot he cut to take the telegraph pole.

"Would you do it again?" I asked Don and Lena.

"Refit the boat, yes, but go back to sea, no!" Don was adamant that his next adventure would be by land.

Peter has more reason than his father to stay on dry land. Some time after arriving in Australia, he took a job as crewman on a prawning trawler. During one trip, the trawler was caught in a violent storm and shipwrecked, finally dumped a long way from the sea, in a mangrove swamp near Shark Bay in Western Australia.

Peter says, after seeing the wind at the height of the storm, peeling paint from the trawler, he has finished with the sea.

"Would you go to sea again, Lena?" I asked.

"If Don wanted to do it again, I'd go with him," she said with a shrug.

When I put the same question to Jonathan his eyes lit up:

"It was great, I'd do it again," he said.

*****

Log Entries

18.5.73

0610	Left Husbands shipyard Southampton. Low visibility.		
0740	Castle Point.		
0830	Off G C Cottages. Set course	243	
0925	Solent Bank.	250	
1115	Needles	254	
1400	St Albans Head	287	
	Fair wind, sails up		
1520	Weymouth.	291	
1600	Tied up Weymouth.		WL 58miles

23.5.73

1115	Left 'Weymouth. Sea medium heavy swell. Wind		west 22 to 26
1315	Portland Bill	230	
1345		275	
1745		275	
1850	Land sighted	275	
1900	Change course to	280	
2000	Brixham outer harbour. At anchor. Engine room shambles, all drawers out and contents in bilge		WL 54miles

No date

0515	Up anchor		
0530	Set Course.	185	Walker log 0
	Dartmouth		
	Start Point		
0830	New course	275	
1145	Eddystone L.H.	275	
1600	Sighted St. Anthony Head		
1630	Falmouth, Drop anchor		WL 75 miles
	At Falmouth take on fuel and water, duty free stores and foodstuffs together with .303 rifle. Bought rubber dingy for diving.		
	High wind caused us to drag anchor which had to be slipped. Later picked up.		

5.6.73   Left Falmouth.

1215	N.E. wind, sails up, course	170	
1250	Walker log in. Set new course	230	

6.6.73

1200	Position 45' 05"N, 8' 00"W.		WL 168 miles.

Auto bilge pump US so main seawater circulating pump now clearing bilges at watch changes.

1500   Change fuel tank to No. 2. Fuel blockage, back to no3. Engine air lock cleared, fuel blockage located and cleared. Back to no. 2 tank. OK.

7.6.73

0600   Course change to   180
Position 46' 30"North, 10' 10"West.   WL 295 miles

8.6.73   Sea up but barometer still steady

0600   Position 43' 52"North, 9' 52"West   WL 453 miles

1500 in port.   One of the blocks on the main sail broken. Sail lowered and stowed for repair

New course.   200

Position, off Finisterre heading parallel with Spanish coast.   WL 523 miles

9.6.73   Still fog, estimate off Portugese coast.

1300   Land sighted. Lecca lighthouse. Decision to put into Leixoes for repairs to mainsail block and bilge pump.

1500   Dropped anchor in Leixoes harbour, waiting customs.

WL 617 miles

13.6.73

1300   Left Leixoes, course   243

Walker log in at 0, change course after 5 miles to 210

Destination Lisbon. Now working 4 hour watch system. This gives eight hours rest and seems much better.

2300   Cabo Mondego beacon sighted, position checks,   39' S0"North, 9' 26"West.
WL 89 miles

0600   Farilhoes rocks sighted. Position check.

Change course towards coast.   WL 100 miles

Followed coast round to entrance to Rio Tejo.

1800   Arrive Lisbon. Q flag up and anchor dropped just off yacht club. Small boat came out after some time telling us that the customs would see us at

0800hrs, on 15.6.73

18.6.73   Lisbon, leave yacht marina

1345   Up to Fort Bucio - Fort St Julias

1455   Set course 240 for three miles   WL 0

1520   Change course to   174

2000   Change course to   180

Position 9' 13"West, 38' 12" North   WL18 miles

19.6.73   Position with 56 miles on log 37' 40" North, 9' 8" West. Course   180

0800	Suspect I have missed Cap St Vincent	
	Change course to 90	
1200	Position by DF, change course to 100 Log reads 143 miles	
1350	Off Tangier, course 95	
	Fix from Pt. Cires	
1500	New course 35	
1610	Pt. Carmeno on port side	
1730	Alongside in destroyer pens in Gibralter.	WL 185 miles

30.6.73 Gibralter   WL 0

1200	Left harbour, set course for Straits and then destination Casablanca	
1400	Thick sea mist, blowing hooter at 3 min intervals	
1600	Fog cleared and off Pt. Cires	WL 20
1915	Off Pta. Malatalon	WL 40
2030	Cape Espartel	WL 52

1.7.73

0200	Off El Araich, course 200	WL 83

3.7•73 Arrive Casablanca

2000	First docking in dark, all OK	WL 200 miles

2.7.73 Casablanca. Asked to leave because we carry a 303 rifle (declared)

1030	Log at 0 next destination Canary Islands	
2359	Position 33' 7"North, 9' 15" West.	
	Course 215	WL 89 miles

4.7.73 Coming up to Conception Bank,

1350	Not Conception Bank navigation error assumed position.	
1800	Course correction towards west and Ferventura.	

5.7.73 Above island not coming up.
        DF sight on Las Palmas shows direction

1530	Heading towards beacon 290	
2000	Light sighted	
2100	More lights flashing but unable to identify	
2200	Close on shore but decide to steam back and forward till daylight.	
2210	Explosion in engine room. Small fire extinguished, turned out to be 1 gall can of Jiser cleaning fluid	
2250	now all OK.	

6.7.73

0800 Canaries	Daylight position indentified as Pt.Arinaga on southern end of Grand	
0830	Walker log tangled with prop	
0915	Log untangled. Went under ship with diving gear, again all OK.	
0920	Make way towards Las Palmas	
1330	Arrive Las Palmas and into outer harbour. La Luz.	
	Hooked onto buoy	WL 626

17.7.73	Left les Palmas The Canaries		
1315	Up sails, , course	200	WL 0
2359	Main gen set US, dismantled found piece of brazing brass in pot giving same result as siezure, removed same, set OK		
18:7.73	Course 200		
	Foot of Mizzen gaff broken		WL 45
	Down for repairs. Deck loaded with F. fish		
I9.7.73	Position 24' 55" North, 18' 15" West.		
0400	Course	242	WL 255
20.7.73	Position 22' 51" North, 22' 55"West.		
	Course	242	WL 414
2000 .	Engine water temp up. Main circ pump US. pump changed		
	P 21' 42" N, 24' 10" W		WL 520
21.7.73	P 20' 51" N, 22' 50" W		
			WL 568
22.7.73	P 18' 55" N, 25' 55" W		
			WL 731
	All OK		
23.7.73	P 16' 18" N, 29' 0" W		
			WL 968
1600	Mizzen gaff repaired and back up, making fair way in calm sea engine and sail		
24.7.73	P 14' 22" N, 30' 45" W		WL 1112
1600	New course	270	
25.7.73	P 12' 45" N, 34' 1" W		WL 1273
1600	Course	285	
	All OK		
26.7.73	P 12' 45" N, 34' 22" W		WL 1436
	Course	285	
27.7.73	P 12' 45" N, 35' 57" W		WL 1519
	Course	285	
	Approx half way across, fuel situation very good in fact better than I dared to hope for.		
28.7.73	P 12' 6" N, 38' 15" W		WL 1642
2359	Course	290	
	Walker log line caught in rope from mizzen sail, untangled and sorted out in ten mins. all OK		
29.7.73	P 12' 29" N, 43' 19" W.		WL 1889
	Course	290	
	Weather close but not as warm as I expected. All OK		

30.7.73	P12' 32" N, 46' 19" W		WL 2035
	Course	290	
	P12' 45" N 48' 46" W.		WL 2180
	Course	290	
I.8.73	P 12' 51" N, 50' 0" W		WL 2251
	Course	290	
2.8.73	P 13' 2" N 52' 49" W		WL 2400
	Course	290	
	Change to No 5 fuel tank, fuel situation very good.		
3.8.73	P 13' 9" N, 55' 18" W		WL 2549
	Course, slight alteration	280	
4.8.73	P 13' 57" N, 58' 18" W		WL 2698
	P. causing concern believe as above steering 300		
	Broken sheet on mizzen sail		
	Reaffirmed position.		
5.8.73	P 9' 11" N 58' 13" W.		WL 2893
	Course	300	
	Echo graph shows sea bed rising 50 fathoms. Assume we are somewhere off River Orinocco because of trees and weed floating in sea.		

6.8.73

0001	we have sighted what we think is Trinidad because of oil rigs but must steam around for daylight.	
0700	Position off Trinidad, Galeota Pt. Decision to pass through the Serpents Mouth.	
1650	Off Serpents Mouth OK	
1800	Problem with auto bilge pump so at anchor off Bonasse. Local fishermen came out to us.	WL 3045

7.8.73	Up anchor and on to Port Fortin	
1030	Arrive P Fortin OK	WL 14
	Repairs and refuel	

10.8.73	Left Port Fortin for Port of Spain	
1030		
1640	Arrive Port of Spain no problems.	WL 70

13.8.73	Left Port of Spain Trinidad for St Georges Grenada.	
1300	Weather dull and squally. The Planesman blew us a farewell salute.	
1700	Passing through Bocas del Dragon into Caribbean Sea	
	Course	310
2000	Engine overheated. Main circ pump again. Fitted reserve and carry on. Sea heavy	

14.8.73

0800	Alongside in St Georges harbour		WL 96

22.8.73

1100	Left St Georges harbour just as Cunard Adventurer arrived.		
	Set course for Caracas Venezuela	246	

23.8.73 P 11° 6" N, 64' 39" W

1430	Passed Isle of Margarita		

24.8.73

0600	Landfall, assume position off Pt. Chospa, propose to		
	follow coast westerly to La Guaira		
1800	In La Guaira harbour alongside		WL 350

30.8.73

0700	Left La Guaira course		284
1200	Change course	300	WL 61
1930	Anchor dropped 5 F		WL 92

31.8.73

0600	Up anchor		
1530	Curacao Stb side		WL 163

1.9.73

0100	Change course	268	WL 285
1300	Aruba Port side		WL 355

2.9.73

0230	Change course	245	WL 400

3.9.73

0100	Course	245	WL 500
2100	Course 245 off Pt Colombia		WL 615

4.9.73

1900	Anchor off Pt Canoas so that we can get into	Cartagena in daylight, have
pilot book but no chart		of harbour
	WL 670	

5.9.73

0600	Up anchor and creep along coast		
1700	At last alongside club de posh in Cartegena		
	Repairs and relax in Cartegena.		WL 710

19.9.73

1500	Left Cartegena		
1800	Into open sea course	255	
	Destination Panama Canal		

20.9.73 Course 255

	Stop and swim in clear blue flat sea.		WL 130

21.9.73

1000	Off Colon entering canal traffic system	WL 245
1130	Into Colon harbour met by U.S, harbour boat. Clear customs and for the present moored to buoy WL 254	

22.9.73   Moved to Cristobal Yacht club mooring awaiting Canal transit,

25.9.73

0730	Pilot on board for canal transit, clear day, up anchor and making for first lock
1030	First lock OK
1130	Rain heavy and visibility very low
1330	Circling round buoy waiting for rain to clear. Pilot uncertain keeps looking at his book
1430	Calabra Cut still raining
1500	Electrical trouble in engine room due to fact that every thing wet through with the rain
1900	Through Canal dropped anchor about 4 miles out from Balboa Distance travelled 40 miles.
	Repairs to electrical system and propeller and waiting for money from Australia.

20.10.73

1600	Left Panama with pilot on board	
1710	Pilot to boat on our own now. Destination Esmereldas.	
	Course	149

21.10.73   New course   161

	P 79' 20" W, 7' 17" N.	WL 95
	Sea heavy	
1700	Main bolts holding V.P. propeller both sheared	WL 97
	Aft. engine room deck up and welded bolts alongside existing ones	
2000	Prop. works OK	
2400	Course	170
	P 6' 39"N, 79' 21" W	WL 130

22.10.73   Sea still heavy

0800	P 5' 57" N, 79' 25" W	WL 175
2000	Course	160 WL 250

23.10.73   Weather improvement, course   155

1200	P 3' 6" N, 79' 34" W.	WL 344
1600	Course	260 WL 394

24.10.73   Course   210

0800	Position off coast just up from Esmereldas, talking to fishermen who suggested we follow them in as the harbour is tricky at low water.
2100	At anchor Esmereldas WL 520
	Repairs spares and fuel

2.11.73	Up anchor	
1600	Left Esmereldas with intention of calling on	Galapagos Isles.
	Wind 18 to 22. sea white tops, sky overcast.	
3.11.73	Course 253	
	P 0' 42" N, 81' 14" W.	WL 95
	Wind dropping 14 to 18 NE	
4.11.73	Course 253	
0800	P 0' 14" N, 83' 43" W	WL 240
1800	Mast head light inoperative	
5.11.73	Crossed Equator	
0400	P 0' 6" 5, 85' 40" W.	
0800	Fuel trouble due to Esmereldas fuel	WL 369
5.11.73	Course 253	
1600	P 0' 28" S, 87' 23" W.	WL 448
6.11.73	Position uncertain	
1200	Believe underestimated drift. Recalculation.	
	New course 328	
	Should have sighted Galapagos by now.	WL 617
7.11.73	Further course change to 360	WL 662
1200	Sighted land believed Isabela	
1600	Following west coast of Isabela to find suitable anchorage to repair masthead lamp and rest.	
1800	At anchor in quiet bay near another fishing boat, did a little business with them for a little water,	
	Isabela, a great big volcanic nothing, went ashore, saw seals iguanas and five trees.	WL 750
8.11.73	Up anchor	
1900	Left Galapagos Bay of Elizabeth as darkness fell,	
	when clear set course for 269	
	Mizzen sail up.	
9.1173	**Day 1, foresail and staysail up.**	
1200	P 1' 00" S, 93' 10" W	WL 114
	Stop engine and check oil	
	Course 268	
10.11.73	Day 2, Mainsail and topsail up.	
1200	P 11 12" S, 96' 02" W	WL 275
	Course 269	
11.11.73	Day 3, Mizzen topsail up, now under full sail but with little effect as wind very slight.	
1200	P 1' 51" S, 99' 04" W.	WL 410
	Course 267	
2330	Engine fuel trouble due to dirty fuel	

12.11.73	**Day 4.**		
0130	Engine fuel trouble clear.		
	New course	265	
1200	P 102' 03" W, 2' 38" S.		WL 592
13.11.73	**Day 5**		
	Course	265	
1200	P 105' 05" W, 3' 58" S		WL 757
14.11.73	**Day 6**		
	Course	265	
1200	P 107' 42" W, 3' 58" S.		WL 923
15.11.73	**Day 7,**		
	Course	265	
1200	P 110' 52" W, 4' 00" S.		WL 1089
	All sails now up		
1730	Engine stopped and try on sails, but wind dropped to below 6 mph.		
1930	Back on engine		
16.11.73	**Day 8**		
	Course	265	
1200	P 113' 25" W, 4' 52" S		WL 1235
	What little wind there is now is from the east and therefore astern, foresail lowered as it is just		flapping.
17.11.73	**Day 9,**		
	Course	265	
0100	Navigation lights US, will look in morning.		
1200	P 116' 42" W 5' 23" S		WL 1399
1400	Problem with Nav. lights at top junction box making difficult because of roll of ship. Everything prepared for tomorrow, average speed now 164 miles per day.		
18.11.73	**Day 10,** course	265	
1000	Temporary repairs to Nav. lights now OK		
1200	P 119' 36" W, 6' 16" S.		WL 1555
	Distance last 24 hours 156 miles		
1400	Stop engine to check oil. Start immediately.		
19.11.73	**Day 11,** course	265	
1100	Engine stopped with intention of sail only		WL 1712
		WLS 0	
	WLS = Small Walker log this being better at lower speeds. Wind speed l0+		
1200	P 122' 24" W, 5' 37" S		WLS 3
	Distance over last 24 hours 167 miles.		
1400	Now engine cool oil change and injector change		

| 2000 | Start engine, decided to use engine at night, this helps to keep up the batts. which are necessary for lights. | WLS 42 |

20.11.73. Day 12, course 265

0215	Air lock in diesel. Spent ages looking and traced fault to filter on front of engine although can see nothing. Dismantled whole thing and put a fibre washer beneath the butterfly nut that holds the filter bowl in place.	
0515	Bleed one more time, this time with success but don't feel too confident.	
1200	P 124' 54" W, 6' 16" S.	WL 1851
	Engine stop, under sail.	WLS 42
1300	Wind 10 to 12	

21.11.73 Day 13, course 260

| 1200 | P 127' 5" W, 6' 30" S. | WL 1940 |
| 1500 | Squalls | WLS 10 |

22.11.73. Day 14, course 260

	Wind improving	
1100	Stop engine, sail only	
1200	P 129' 10" W 7' 20" S	WL 2040
		WLS 4
	Distance over last 24 hours 96	
1330	Topsail pin sheared, mainsail lowered to weld new shackle back in position.	
1500	Topsail back up, mainsail back up	

23.11.73 Day 15, course 265

1200	P 131' 28" W, 7' 20" S.	WL 2140
		WLS 17
	Alteration to foresail complete. Foresail now square rig on a boom.	
1330	Up and sailing good. Engine stop and sail on.	

24.11.73 Day 16, course 265

	After sailing through night	WLS 104
0900	Start engine	
1200	P 133' 36" W, 7' 51" S	WL 2164
1300	Stop engine back to sail	

25.11.73 Day 17, course 265

	Continue with a mixture of sail and engine	
1200	P 135` 48" W, 8' 07" S	WL 2293
		WLS 80

26.1I.73 Day 18, course 265

1200	Sighted land (Falsi Huki)	
	Change course to	297
1630	Drop anchor in Baie de Vaipace Ua Huka. Rest for tonight.	

27.11.73

0800	Up anchor and staysail and on to Nuka Hiva		
1100	Arrive Nuka Hiva Baie de Taiohae. Drop anchor find local customs etc..		WL 2390

29.11.73

Rest and repair, take on a little fuel. (very expensive $25 for a 50 gall drum.

5.12.73

0600	Up anchor, foresail and staysail.		
	Course	170	WL 0
1130	Drop anchor Motia Takahe Ua Pou		WL 30
	Rest and meet local people. Went hunting and eat fresh meat (Goats)		

8.12.73

	Up anchor, foresail and staysail.		
1800	Set course for Tahiti	249	WL 0
2000	Mizzen sail up with M topsail		

Day 1

	course	249	
0930	Mainsail up, sail and engine together, not much		wind.
1200	P 142' 05" W 10' 10" S.		WL 126

Day 2

	course	**248**	
	P 144' 18" W, 11' 14" S.		WL 288

Day 3

	course	248	
	P 146' 43" W, 13' 6" S.		WL 452

Day 4

	course	248	
0800	Course correction	232	
1200	P 148' 51" W, 14' 24" S		WL 624
1400	Course change	180	

13.12.73

	course	180	
0800	Land sighted. Tetiaroa.		
	Change course to	170	WL 774
1200	Change course to	165	
1630	Enter Papeete harbour with pilot.		
1700	Drop anchor		WL 805
	At anchor in Papeete harbour "World fuel crisis". No fuel.		
	Painting ship. Christmas and New Year seen in on board British ship Blue Rover RFA supply ship to Royal Yacht. Fueled up.		

21.1.74 Day 1, up anchor, left Papeete.

1530	Set course for Raratonga	262	

22.1.74 Day 2, course

		262	
1200	P 151' 32" W 18' 22" S.		WL 131
1400	Overtaken by cruise ship Monterey		

23.1.74	Course	262	
1200	P 153' 57" W, 181 33" S		WL 286
1300	Course change	255	

24.1.74 Day 3, course 262

0700	Dynamo drive coupling broken- stop engine		
0745	Repaired, start engine		
1200	P 156' 16" W 20' 16" S		WL 422
	Noon till noon 163 miles.		

25.1.74 Day 4, course 262

Noon	Working on DF for Raratonga		WL 622
1300	Main gaff broken, mainsail lowered		
1700	Land sighted, change course	310	WL 676
1900	Off Raratonga, but due to heavy seas and darkness		
	dare not try to land today		

26.1.74 Day 5

0600	Through the small gap in reef and alongside.		
0645	Stop engine		
	Raratonga, make gaff and take on fuel.		

12.2.74 Day 1,

0845	Set to sea through the reef on course for New Zealand Northern Isle.		
0900	Walker log in, course	252	
	Sea heavy, wind 22mph from SE		

13.2.74 Day 2, course 252

Noon	Approx. position l62'22", 23'38'		WL 163
	Sky overcast with occasional heavy squalls		

14.2.74 Day 3, course 252

Noon	P 164' 18"W, 23'48"S.		WL 311
	Still squalls and fairly big sea but becoming calmer		

15.2.74 Day4, course 252

	Overcast, position by DR 167' 44"W, 25' 10"S.	WL 466	

16.2.74 Day5, course 252

Noon	P 168' 52"W, 26' 15"S.		WL 623
1300	Change to No 2 fuel tank		
1310	Mainsail repaired and reset.		Wind SE
1410	Foresail sheet broken at topmast		

17.2.74 Day 6, course 252

Noon	P 171' 23"W, 28' 1"S.		WL 782

18.2.74 Day7, course 252

Noon	P 173' 59"W, 29' 22"S.		WL 946

19.2.74 Day 8, course 250

			WL 1104
	P 176' 05"W, 30' 46"S.		
	Barometer 1019		

20.2.74 **Day 9,** course   250

Barometer 1022

P 178' 25"W, 32' 16"S   WL 1262

Daily mileage 158

21.2.74 **Day 10,** course   250

Barometer 1025

Noon   P 179' 57"W, 33' 48"S.   WL1425

Daily mileage 243

22.2.74 **Day 11,** course   250

Barometer 1024

0200   Breakdown. Steering chain pulley pulled from wheelhouse deck. had to remove old bolts and refit new ones.

0300   Repair OK but chain still very slack

1200   Position by DR no sun sight possible

P 177' 13"E, 33' 25"S,   WL 1597

2100   Spotted light believed Mokohinua

23.2.74

Course   205

Barometer 1020

1200   Not Mokohinua unable to find likeness on charts.

1300   Called Auckland radio because DF giving adverse readings, asked for fix, none available but ZLDQ advised northerly course along coast.

1430   Sighted large island off coast. Culvier Isle.

1630   Decided to drop anchor in cove near Culvier Isle lighthouse.

1700   At anchor. Lighthouse man came out, will continue to Auckland in morning. Anchor watch.   WL 1680

24.2.74

1000   Up anchor set course for Channel Isle. Quiet crossing.

1900   Arrived Auckland, alongside Marsden wharf. Customs formalities all OK.   WL 62.

10.3.74

0830   Left Auckland

0900   Off Rangitotto Isle

1020   Sails up Walker log in   WL 0

Course   360

1600   Drop anchor in lee off Little Barrier Isle.   WL 39

11.3.74

0630   Up anchor,

Course   320

1130   Take in Walker log, then through the bay, 15 miles   WL 73

1430	Alongside at No 3 Fertiliser wharf Whangarei, Customs etc.		

15.3.74 Day 1

1300	Left Whangarei by the Royal Passage to the sea. 12 miles		
1500	Walker log in		WL 0
1700	Set course	300	
	Poor Knights Isle off starboard		
2000	Barometer 997		WL 29
2200	Off Cape Brett		WL 51

16.3.74 Day 2, position off NZ coast,

	N cape sighted.		WL 149
1400	Bar 992 going down		
1800	Set course off N Cape	290	WL 165

17.3.74 Day 3, barometer 990

	NE wind heavy big sea.		
Noon	Course	290	WL 278
1400	Mainsail torn and taken down. Sea rough.		

18.3.74 Day 4, course 290

0130	Foresail sheet broken have to take sail down; also damaged.		
	Sea still rough barometer 996		
Noon	Position by DR because of sea.		
	P 168' 00"E, 33' 48"S.		WL 430

19.3.74 Day 5, weather improving.

	Barometer 1002,		
	Course	280	
Noon	P 164' 11"E, 33' 51"S		WL 586
	Made good last 24 hours 156 miles. Start repairing sails, main up but reefed in first position.		

20.3.74 Day 6. course 270

0400	Barometer 1005		WL 706
	Wind now north.		
Noon	P 168' 01"E, 35' 00"S.		W'L 730
	Made good in last 24 hours 144 miles.		
1400	Foresail sheet repaired and sail back up.		

21.3.74 Day 7, course 270

0200	Bar 1017		WL 826
Noon	P 159' 43"E, 35' 30"S.		WL 877
1300	Mainsail repairs complete, full sail up		
	Mizzen topsail up		
	Made good today 147 miles		

22.3.74 Day 8, course 280

	Barometer 1020		

Noon	P 156' 05"E, 37' 40"S		WL 1042
12.30	Course correction	300	
23.3.74	**Day 9,** course	300	
	Barometer 1018		
Noon	P 153' 20"E, 37' 00"S		WL 1228
1300	Change course	305	
24.3.74	**Day 10,** course	305	
	Barometer 1017		
Noon	Land sighted Green Cape lighthouse.		WL 1365
1500	Alongside at Eden		
	Whilst in Eden slipped ship check hull and anti foul, all found good.		
	Waiting for weather.		
15.4.74			
0400	Let go buoy. Bar 1016		
	Head for entrance of Twofold Bay.		WL in.
0500	Course	095	
0700	Course	190	
	Off Green Cape light.		WL 22
1040	Off Gabo Isle		
	Course	277	
1400	Off Point Hicks		
	Course	285	WL 73
16.4.74	Bar 1019 course	270	
1215	Off Cliffy Isle		WL 222
1445	Off Wilsons Prom		WL 250
2000	Round Wilsons Prom		
	Off Cape Woolamai		WL 306
17.4.74	Bar 1014 course	315	
0400	Off Cape Schanck		WL 334
0600	Pt Lonsdale light sighted		
	set course for same		WL 356
0745	Coming in through Lonsdale rip		
0810	Alongside lifeboat station Queenscliff		WL 361
	Tied up and walked round to see if it is possible to moor in creek.		
0900	Local fisherman piloted us up creek, made fast Queenscliff.		

No Log entries after Queenscliff

END

Author

Paul England

Paul was born and educated in England.
During the 40s and 50s he served in the Royal Navy.
As an electronics engineer he worked in America, UK,
Europe and Australia.
In 1974 he transferred to Australia with his family.
Now retired, he lives on the south coast of NSW.
Since retirement he has been kept fully occupied
writing children's books and short stories, painting in
watercolours and landscaping his garden.
Several of his short stories have been published in
national magazines and local newspapers.
Over the last few years he has written six books,
'Zoom One, 'Commando' and 'Frogger'- the first three
books in the children's series "Knights of Bonalla',
'Voyage of a Lifetime' - which was first published by
L&R Hartley and now published as an Ebook and
paperback, 'Tunguska', a general Sci Fi based on an
actual incident, and 'The Punishment', an anthology of
short stories.